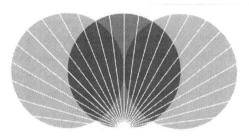

Aligned: Returning to God's Perfect Peace in an Anxious World

May you find your soul's peace in the LORD as you become aligned with his heart!

♡, **KASEY SHULER**

Kasey Shuler

Cover Design by Seth Nickerson
Interior formatting by Kim Li
Font families used: Grandway, PT Serif
ISBN: 978-1-7334680-2-2

To Mattox, Ellie, and Sara, who keep me in line.

"You keep him in perfect peace whose mind is stayed on you, because he trusts in you." —*Isaiah 26:3*

CONTENTS

About the Author vi

Introduction vii

Session 1: Our State of Disintegration 1

Session 2: Redefining Perfect Peace 30

Session 3: The Path to Realignment 58

Session 4: Name What You Do Not Know 87

Session 5: Live What You Know...................................116

Session 6: Learn to Let the Rest Go 145

Session 7: Take the Next Step 175

Epilogue 205

Appendix 207

Acknowledgements 215

About the Author

Kasey Shuler is an author, personal trainer, and co-founder of the *Joyful Health Collective*. Her mission is to help women find lasting health by starting with grace and finding joy walking by faith. She lives with her husband and two daughters in Athens, Georgia, and would love to connect with you at *joyfulhealth.co*, or on Instagram *@kaseybshuler* and *@joyfulhealthco*.

You can find a video companion course for *Aligned* with teachings from Kasey at *joyfulhealth.co/aligned*.

Introduction

"What am I getting myself into?" I fretted as I read the waiver at the chiropractor's office. It was my first experience, and I was a little thrown off by the doom and gloom wording. I weighed the cost of permanent damage to my spine versus living with upper back pain. The possibility of a pain-free existence trumped the probability of irreversible injury. I took a breath, and signed on the dotted line. What happened next has stuck with me, and is the backbone of this study. As the chiropractor instructed me to sit down, she explained her philosophy: my body was already good at healing, and her job was to restore the flow and communication through spinal adjustment. Something distant and deep clicked in my spirit.

I've lived with anxiety on the fringes of my soul since as long as I can remember. One prominent memory from my childhood is the time my dad forgot to put the drain plug in the family boat and I thought we were going to sink, *Titanic* style. Decades of worry over being drowned, running late, and falling short have left me scattered, frayed, and tired of drifting. The chiropractor visit fell at a time ripe for receiving. The parallel message I perceived from the Lord was: "I have already given you what you need for life and peace in my Word, confirmed by my promises. Whenever you feel disoriented, return to me. Trust me. Leave your worries at the door. I'll remind you of my ways, and your heart will fall in line. I am your center. The peace you seek has been right here all along." All my worries melted away. I knew beyond a shadow of a doubt these words were from God because of three things:

1. **Peace:** They left me with a sense of peace I haven't found in the world.

2. **Presence:** They fulfilled my yearnings from the past, hopes for the future, and desire to be fully present.

3. **Promise:** These words aligned with His promises in Scripture.

I had been striving for peace, when all I needed was to return to God and His promises. I knew this message wasn't just for me. My eyes were opened, and I saw alignment everywhere.

Do any of these statements resonate with you?

- "My angry outbursts feel so out of character. This isn't who I am."

- "If I can just get my head above water, I'll be able to breathe again."

- "I don't know what decision to make, and I'm so stressed over it."

- "That doesn't align with my core values."

I'll bet you have at least one issue on which you feel misaligned. Maybe it's a relationship, a job, or a season of hardship. It could be major indecision fatigue, a sinking regret from the past, or a literal pain in the neck. You realize it's a problem because the thought of confronting it sends your body into a tailspin, heart rate accelerating and stomach in knots. You know there's an answer but can't quite figure it out. All you know is, you just want it resolved. Recognize this emotional state as a cue to pause, take a step back, and see what's not fitting together like it should.

I see this reflected in my three-year-old, who is learning to buckle the chest straps on her car seat. She will try to shove the two crooked pieces together until her little face turns red and trembles with frustration. I gently lean over and say, "First you get the pieces aligned, and then you push them together." Click!

Jesus left us this gift in John 14:27: "Peace I leave with you; my peace I give to you. Not as the world gives do I give to you. Let not your hearts be troubled, neither let them be afraid." *Aligned* is about returning to the perfect peace Jesus has already given us. And once we do...click! We may not be perfect yet, but we can rest in His perfect peace. Maybe all it takes is realignment.

The Path from Anxious to Aligned

My hope as you travel through each session of this study is to move from the column on the left to the column on the right:

Anxious	Aligned
Chaotic	Calm
Tense	Relaxed
Uncertain	Assured
Striving	Surrendered
Panicked	Able to Pause
Shakey	Stable
Dreadful	Trusting

If anxiety is like flailing in the water, being aligned is to put your feet down on the rock of God's promises. If. You have no idea where to start, this book will help you connect with the truth of the Lord's sure and steady reality.

1. **Our State of Disintegration:** In Session 1, we will talk about what causes worry and divides our minds. If we are whole in Christ, what are the messages of culture that cause disconnection from who we are in the presence of God? Anxiety is common, but it doesn't have to be normal.

2. **Redefining Perfect Peace:** Session 2 paints the picture of perfect peace of the Lord so we not only know what we are looking for and that it exists, but is ready and waiting for us to find.

3. **The Path to Realignment:** Session 3 marks the path of realignment with God's perfect peace: how to continually live in a state of alignment, seeking adjustments when needed.

4. **Name What You Do Not Know:** Session 4 helps name and tame what you don't know. A marker of anxiety is a general sense of tension, apprehension, or dread, so we are going to entrust what we cannot know into God's hands.

5. **Live What You Know:** Session 5 directs us to walk what we know according to God's Word. Integrity is doing what you believe. This week will guide you to stand on rock-solid beliefs so you can put them into practice and leave anxiety in the dust.

6. **Learn to Let the Rest Go:** Session 6 allows you to let the rest go. Once we define what is eternally part of us, we are free to open our hands in surrender to following Jesus, no holding back.

7. **Take the Next Step:** Session 7 encourages action, the final piece to the puzzle. Once your priorities are stacked rightly and you've let go of the weight of sin and shame, you can take the next step. Go in peace, walk humbly with your God, be a peacemaker, and continue with the seasons.

This study may take seven weeks, but once you learn the steps, you will be able to quickly implement them into your life whenever you feel spiritually off-center.* May this be a study to serve you in hiding God's Word in your heart as an anchor of hope and place of peace.

Note that this study is not a treatment for anxiety. If symptoms of anxiety have a central place in your day, please consult a professional and get the help you need.

How to Use this Study

Divide the content into seven consecutive weeks, or spread them out according to your study needs or a group's schedule.

Read

Each week has four days of a devotional, along with a verse and seven questions to dig deeper. Please see these questions as invitations rather than expectations. If you can't think of an answer, you may simply write, "Lord, I am trusting you to reveal this to me." Let this simple prayer open your eyes and ears to what He wants to show you about this topic as your day unfolds. You'll also notice that one question is highlighted on each day's study. Be prepared to talk about these questions when you get together with a group for discussion on day five.

Practice

At the end of the questions, you'll see a final exercise to integrate God's Word into your life in a more holistic way. Feel free to use these exercises with a group as well.

Pray

You'll have an opportunity to write a short prayer to reflect on what God has shown you.

To follow up the written prayer (which clarifies the thoughts in your mind), a centering prayer gives you the chance to focus on the meditations of your heart. Centering prayer is simple, and there are no real rules. The point is to strengthen inner peace by sitting in stillness with the Lord.

Here's how: find a place where you won't be disturbed, and resume a position where your body can be relaxed and your mind remain aware. Close your eyes or gaze at something neutral, and open your heart to meet with God and align your spirit with His. Using a word, phrase, or image from that day's Scripture, practice holding it in your mind as you let the rest of your thoughts go.

You may also use your breath, returning to an inhale, exhale rhythm. This is an anchor point to return to when your thoughts stray. Try for as little as two minutes. Set a timer so you won't be thinking about the clock, and then as you settle in, take as long as you need.

As you continue in dedicated intention, you will notice yourself releasing dependence on strict formalities. You just might notice yourself doing a moment of centering prayer without thinking during a stressful time in your day. And this is the goal: to increase your meetings with the Lord, expanding your peace of presence as you become more aligned with Him.

Recap and Watch

On Day 5 of each week, you'll have a chance to recollect what God has been teaching you to reinforce it. You may also access video teachings designed for personal study or to watch as a group before discussion questions. You can find these videos at *joyfulhealth.co/aligned* or use the QR code below:

I'd love to hear from you as you begin. Would you send an email to me at **hi@kaseybshuler.com** with the subject line "I'm ready to be aligned with peace" as a sign of your commitment, for God's glory, and for mutual joy?

Here's my prayer for you as you begin your journey:

"May the God of hope fill you with all joy and peace in believing, so that by the power of the Holy Spirit you may abound in hope." —Romans 15:13

Grace and peace,

Kasey Shuler

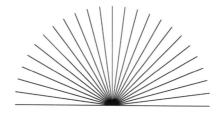

Session 1: Our State of Disintegration

The whole world at your fingertips, the ocean at your door.
That Funny Feeling by Bo Burnham

Day 1: The Truth Behind Being True to You

The anxiety is mounting. I lost a major chunk of this devotional to the great unknown and have spent hours rewriting this exact page over and over to no avail. I'm buckling under the pressure of deadlines and the accusations are loud: "You've wasted months. You could have been done by now. You're so irresponsible." This is who I stake myself on: being responsible. I can feel the tension in my body: I'm short on breath, my chest feels tight, and I just might cry. Who we believe we are matters. It literally affects our matter, our physical experience and lens on life. But we can choose the voices we listen to. We can listen to the half-truths and become anxious, or we can pause, listen to the whole truth of God's voice, and come back to who we are.

The question is: who are we? Authenticity is one of our society's most prized values: "be true to *you*," the influencers say. And if you aren't sure who you are, marketing has plenty of solutions on the table: "You can be anyone! If you work hard enough, you can be rich! If you do the right diet, you can be a size two!" But I've found too many holes in this plot. What happens when the identity you're leaning on falls apart? What if you identify as a student and then graduate? What if you identify as a sound steward of your body but become ill? Or what if...you achieve it all but still feel hollow? In that space of disillusioned loss, anxiety rushes in like a great flood. But there is a rock to stand on, an unshakable solid pillar of peace that has always been, is there now, and will always be.

Whether you've been the disappointment, made a major life shift, or succeeded as a CEO, none if this is the true you. You can neither create truth with your choices, nor compromise your innate value with blunders. If you want to be true to you, lean in and listen up: *you already are.* God loves you as you are now and promises to use *all things* to work together for your salvation. And that's what matters. Being "true to you" as a Christian means being true to the person you already are in Christ: "But now thus says the LORD, he who created you, O Jacob, he who formed you, O Israel: 'Fear not, for I have redeemed you; I have called you by name, you are mine.'" (Isaiah 43:1). You are His. Be true to that. Come back to the peace that is Yours in Christ. Let's become aligned with Him.

"But now thus says the LORD, he who created you, O Jacob, he who formed you, O Israel: 'Fear not, for I have redeemed you; I have called you by name, you are mine.'" —Isaiah 43:1

Write this verse below:

"BUT NOW THUS SAYS THE LORD, HE WHO CREATED YOU, O

JACOB, HE WHO FORMED YOU, O ISRAEL: "FEAR NOT, FOR I

HAVE REDEEMED YOU; I HAVE CALLED YOU BY NAME, YOU ARE

MINE". ISAIAH 43:1

1. What words would you use to describe who you are? You
   may refer to a personality test that has resonated with you,
   or pick out a few words from this list below to help you form
   your answer:

Dependable   Assertive   Fun
Generous   Supportive   (Unique)
(Loyal)   (Growth-oriented) Thoughtful
Courageous   (Self-reliant)   (Honest)
Adaptable   Encouraging   (Cautious)

RESPONSABLE, LOYAL, GROWTH-ORIENTED, SELF-RELIANT,

UNIQUE HONEST, CAUTIOUS FEARFUL, PATIENT, INDEPENDENT,

DISCIPLINE, JUDGEMENTAL, SHY, QUIET, INTROVERT, ORGANIZED

2. What feelings does the phrase "be true to you" bring up?

ANNOYED, IRRITATED BULLSHIT,

3. Describe a time when you felt anxious or disoriented because you weren't in alignment with the person you thought you were:

I FELT ANXIOUS BECAUSE I WORRY EXCESIVELY ABOUT MY HEALTH. I FEEL TERRIFIED IF I GET SICK HERE AND I AM BY MYSELF AND ALSO DON'T HAVE MONEY TO PAY THE HEALTH CARE THAT IS EXPENSIVE.

4. Look at Isaiah 43:1. This passage comes after Israel is disciplined for straying from God (see Isaiah 42:18-25). The Lord said He created Jacob, He created our ancestors, He created the line of God's people. When you attempt to create your own identity, what voices are you listening to? Who does God create you to be according to Isaiah 43:1?

TO CREATE MY OWN IDENTITY I LISTEN TO MYSELF AND OTHER PEOPLES VOICES (THEIR COMMENTS ABOUT ME)
GOD
↳ NOT BE FEARFUL, BE CHOSEN (HIS DAUGHTER), AND PERFECT IN SPIRIT (REDEEM), NOT TO BE FEARFUL, NOT TO BE FEARFUL.

5. God called Jacob "Israel" after he wrestled with God in Genesis 32:28. Israel means "struggles with God." Becoming who God created us to be is a process. We don't find ourselves by looking within, but by wrestling with God. It is not *what* we struggle with but *who* we wrestle with that

defines us. What piece of your identity are you struggling with right now, and how can you direct your doubts to God?

_____

_____

_____

_____

_____

_____

6. "Do not fear, for I have redeemed you..." In the Bible God tell us not to fear 365 times, once for every day of the year. We may face the unknown each new day, but what we need to know is what God has already said: "I *have* redeemed you" (notice the past tense). You do not need to worry about your choices making or breaking you today. Name what you are afraid of today:

I am afraid of_____.

Now hear God's response: "Do not fear, for I have redeemed you."

7. And finally: "I have called you by your name; you are Mine!" Biblical names are often manifestations of a person's character. You might identify with the core values you listed from question 1. These could change. You might identify with a certain role. Today, you might be called many things:

a friend, a wife, a student, an employee. Name your top three, and follow it up with the unchangeable truth of who you are and will always be:

- _____, for today, and the Lord's always.

- _____, for today, and the Lord's always.

- _____, for today, and the Lord's always.

Look back to the beginning of Isaiah 43:1: "Now this is what the Lord says." In her book *The Broken Way*, Ann Voskamp says, "If we all listen long enough to the voices about who we should be, we grow deaf to the beauty of who we are."[1] During your day, check your fears. Is that what the Lord says? If not, dismiss it as not from Him, and therefore, not for you. Align yourself with the unshakeable truth of who He says you are.

Write a prayer based on today's reflections:

_____

_____

_____

_____

_____

---

[1] Ann Voskamp, *The Broken Way: A Daring Path into the Abundant Life* (Grand Rapids, Michigan: Zondervan, 2016), 183.

Take a few moments to do a centering prayer based on your written prayer. Take a thought, word, or symbol that stands out. Every time your thoughts stray, return to the center of your intention. Remain until you feel satisfied in the Lord and aligned with His peace. Refer to the Introduction pages for more instructions on centering prayer.

Day 2: You Can Do It All! But It Will Break You

When I was in high school, I was president of everything. I was President of Beta Club, Bible study leader, and student council even created a new executive position just for me. My friends joked I was president of the school. But was I happy? I was breaking myself to do it all because I was told I could do anything. I wanted to be a good steward with the gifts God gave me. But I found myself regularly crying from stress overload. My heart was for God, but I was crumbling under the idol of hustle culture: "Wow, you can do it all!" was a high compliment. But "doing it all" doesn't glorify God or make us better people. It made me just plain miserable. Are humans made to burn ourselves out, or are we made for God? Are we made to be God, or to be aligned with Him instead?

My planner may have been overbooked, but I was always thinking about what more significant thing I needed to be doing or where I should be instead. My heart was divided and mind distracted. Charles Stone, author of *Holy Noticing* said our culture of distraction "has resulted in something called continuous partial attention, which means 'to keep a top-level item in focus, and constantly scan the periphery in case something more important emerges."[2] We're always looking for something better than what we have, especially with social media as a showcase for "the better thing you could be doing." But doing more than what God's will prescribes divides us from the peace we have in Christ.

---

[2] Charles Stone, Holy Noticing: The Bible, Your Brain, and the Mindful Space Between Moments (Chicago: Moody Publishers, 2019), 110.

If we knew God's will for our daily planners, we could settle our hearts and release distractions. But wait, He's already told us! "Rejoice always, pray without ceasing, give thanks in all circumstances; for this is the will of God in Christ Jesus for you" (1 Thessalonians 5:16-18). That's it. Nothing between the lines. Doing God's will turns out to be much different (and more freeing) than our idea of right living. You don't need to do it all to please the Lord or make the most of life. What God wants is for us to rejoice, pray, and give thanks. This is our peace. Simple.

"Rejoice always, pray without ceasing, give thanks in all circumstances; for this is the will of God in Christ Jesus for you" —1 *Thessalonians 5:16-18*

Write down the verse <u>as slow as possible</u> below:

_____

_____

_____

1. Have you felt the pressure to do everything? What contributes to that feeling—family background, being a parent, digital media, something else?

_____

_____

_____

2. We often miss God's will for us because we are too busy, too distracted, too afraid to stop, or too afraid to fail. We forget that the Lord doesn't ask us to do more for Him but desires a heart at peace in His presence. In what area of your life are you doing too much apart from the Lord's peace? What are the consequences on your body, your mind, your relationship with God?

   _____

   _____

   _____

3. Let's look at what we need to be doing according to 1 Thessalonians 5:16-18. What is God's will, and how does that contrast with your idea of what He wants?

   _____

   _____

   _____

4. The Church of Thessalonica was persecuted, and yet Paul told them to "rejoice always." What do you have to rejoice in God about, regardless of circumstances? Complete this sentence:

   God, I rejoice in you over...

   _____

   _____

_____

_____

5. "Pray without ceasing" is a surefire way to keep us in the perfect peace of God's presence, even in the middle of an anxiety-ridden world. What does your prayer life look like right now? How does prayer grant you inner peace and direct your steps during your day?

_____

_____

_____

_____

6. "Give thanks in all things." In her book, *The Hiding Place*, Corrie Ten Boom and her sister were housed in a Nazi-run concentration camp when their bunks became infested with bed bugs. While Corrie wondered how they could possibly give thanks in *this* situation, the bed bug infestation kept the guards away so they could have private Bible studies. God is in the business of redemption. What impossible situation can you give thanks for, trusting that God's will is ultimately for our good?

_____

_____

_____

7. The last part of the verse says, "in Christ Jesus for you."
   Contemplate Jesus' life and how He fulfilled the will of God.
   Name one instance where Jesus accomplished God's will
   when it may have been against the grain of society's culture.

_____

_____

_____

_____

Every moment of our day seems like an opportunity to
multitask. Resist and return to a singular focus. You can try this
today by practicing a mindful meal. Pick one meal today where
you can have zero distractions. Take three deep breaths and say,
"What is the will of God?" and then quote 1 Thessalonians 5:16-
18. Repeat the verse as you eat, noticing textures, temperature,
flavor profiles, even giving thanks for those who grew and
harvested the food. As you do so, let God's perfect peace settle
upon you in that moment and as you rise to go about your day
with intention.

Write a prayer based on today's reflections:

_____

_____

_____

_____

Based on our verse for today, take a moment for centering prayer. Choose a word that stuck out to you, and offer it up to the Lord, letting Him plant it into your heart with each breath you take.

Day 3: When Is Enough, Enough?

Anxiety is the product of contemporary ambition. In a world when you can be anyone, do it all, but also need to be true to you, how do we know when enough is enough? In her book, *The Way of Integrity*[3], author Martha Beck shared a story of a successful client who called her in the middle of a roaring party to celebrate a $200 million deal by screaming over the noise into the phone: "YOU KNOW WHAT? IT ISN'T ENOUGH! I THOUGHT IT WOULD BE ENOUGH, BUT IT'S NOT!"

We don't need to chase the world's version of success. $200 million deals, becoming famous, buying a house...all these things are good, but do not promise the peace we were made for. They may, however, leave you with more anxiety. The fallacy the world sells us is that when we make it to the top, we will have arrived. We will have security. But this is an illusion, a forever dangling carrot, a shadow of what Jesus offers.

I can easily look back on many achievements and say that more is not better. When we aim to be better than others, we miss the joy of being ourselves with our God. Ambition is not evil, but self-centered ambition strays from the Lord's design. Instead of following our own deceitful ambitions, may we follow the bigger Kingdom vision. Kingdom ambition is to "aspire to live quietly, and to mind your own affairs, and to work with your hands" (1 Thessalonians 4:11). Glamorous? No. Expected? Certainly not. The way of peace? Absolutely.

---

[3] Martha Beck, The Way of Integrity: Finding the Path to Your True Self (New York: Penguin Life, 2021), 26

Anxiety lies in the pressure to create and maintain your own existence. But friend, you can rest in peace now. Your old self has died, and now you live to Christ. You don't have to prove yourself. God has already proved His love for us in Christ and created us anew. If you've felt pulled apart by others' ideas of success, let this verse settle your soul and reorient your new self to the work of Christ. On the cross, Jesus said, "it is finished." Isn't this enough? Let your anxiety rest at the foot of the cross. Let this be the holy ground from which you stand with Him alone.

Look up multiple translations of 1 Thessalonians 4:11 and write down the interpretation that speaks most to you:

_____

_____

_____

_____

1. Have you ever had a mountaintop experience after achieving your goals and looked around wondering, "is this all there is?" Did your pursuit take from you more than it gave? How did you respond?

_____

_____

_____

_____

2. Consider 1 Thessalonians 4:11. The section heading in the Bible is *A Life Pleasing to God*. Read 1 Thessalonians 4 and write what is pleasing to God:

_____

_____

_____

3. Referring to question one, what life circumstances led you to that goal? Was it your own ambition, someone else's idea of success, or a desire to please God?

_____

_____

_____

4. Take note of the contrast of the different ways to be successful:

Modern Ambition	Biblical Ambition
Be an influencer with global impact	Live quietly
Be connected with powerful people and call others out	Mind your own affairs
Constantly create digital content to become an internet authority	Work with your hands

How does the left side make you feel?

_____

_____

_____

How about the right side?

_____

_____

_____

5. To lead a quiet life does not mean you cannot stand up for what you believe. Paul wrote this letter to the church in response to Timothy's report that the new converts were steadfast.

    But there were rumors circulating that Paul had used manipulation and flattery to win over believers, and here he was writing not only to share the truth, but to encourage the believers not to stir the pot. Instead, he encouraged them to remain spiritually undisturbed. Despite popular visions of success, you do not need to "make a scene" to be seen. Considering the personal pressure for ambition, what would it mean for you to "make it your ambition to live a quiet life"?

_____

_____

_____

_____

_____

_____

6. Far from being gossips that divide the unity of fellowship, Paul called for the Thessalonians to "mind your own affairs," and attend to their own business. Note that he doesn't tell us to respond with "mind your own beeswax!" if someone asks after your state of mind. We are called to diligently pursue our calling with a singular focus on God. What makes it easier to get involved with the life of another rather than to do your own business?

_____

_____

_____

_____

_____

7. Many of the new believers in Thessalonica were artisans, and Paul called them back from spreading the gospel away from home "to work with your hands, as we instructed you, so that you may walk properly before outsiders and be dependent on no one." Compare this behavior with those of Acts 17:21: "Now all the Athenians and the foreigners who lived there would spend their time in nothing except telling

or hearing something new." How can working with your hands produce peace not just for yourself, but for others?

_____

_____

_____

_____

Work done outside of God's design leads to disintegration of the self and society. Before you try to prove yourself in the public sphere, practice the presence of God in private. If your anxiety mutters, "You don't have time for that. You have work to do," turn away and return to God's Word: "Aspire to live quietly, and to mind your own affairs, and to work with your hands, as we instructed you" (1 Thessalonians 4:11).

Write a prayer based on today's work:

_____

_____

_____

Spend a few moments in quiet reflection and centering prayer. Hold a word from the verse today in your mind, bowing your head and letting it rest in your heart. Rise up and give yourself to the Lord.

Day 4: Follow His Heart

"What should I do?" When stricken with indecision, well-wishers often counsel, "It's easy! Just follow your heart!" But considering the words of Jeremiah 17:9, that doesn't seem advisable: "The human heart is the most deceitful of all things, and desperately wicked. Who really knows how bad it is?" (NLT) Following our heart like a Disney princess may not lead to happily ever after. *Sigh.* Following our own sinful heart is to choose the wayward path: fun at first, but only leads to a dead-end. Delighting yourself in the Lord, however, is to align yourself with His desires. His path becomes your path, the one you choose after all.

Which heart will you follow? The old heart of the flesh, vying for its former seat in the center of your life, or the heart of the Lord, who is truly worthy of your worship? The way of the flesh is self-centered, but the way of the Spirit is surrender. Theologian François Fénelon said it best:

> *Anxiety and misgiving proceed solely from love of self. The love of God accomplishes all things quietly and completely; it is not anxious or uncertain. The Spirit of God rests continually in quietness. Perfect love casteth out fear. It is in forgetfulness of self that we find peace. Happy is he who yields himself completely, unconsciously, and finally to God. Listen to the inward whisper of His spirit and follow it—that is enough; but to listen one must be silent and to follow one must yield.*

Here's the truth: we can't fix our hearts. But by faith, we can follow God's heart. Psalm 37:4 says, "Delight yourself in the Lord, and he will give you the desires of your heart." He will put desires in your heart which seek His delight, and these will become your new appetites. I experienced this in my own life when we lived in Seattle, a city I proclaimed I would never leave. But as soon as we got pregnant, a switch flipped. I wanted another car, I wanted suburbia (did I say that out loud?), I wanted to be around family. The Lord gave me new desires to equip me to best love our child. Our sinful heart set on survival is loud, desperate, and resistant to change. But the mind set on the spirit is life and peace. You might be surprised at the joy God gives you when you follow God's heart, step by silent step. Your desires will soon become His, and the path ahead becomes your new happily ever after.

"Delight yourself in the Lord, and he will give you the desires of your heart." —Psalm 37:4

Write down the verse from above, and add either Psalm 37:3 before it, or Psalm 37:5 after it.

_____

_____

_____

_____

_____

1. What are your thoughts on the phrase "follow your heart"?

_____

_____

_____

_____

_____

2. Do you have any personal experience with this advice?

_____

_____

_____

_____

3. David, who was called "a man after God's own heart," is the author of Psalm 37. According to this Psalm, what is God's heart? Write a verse for reference.

_____

_____

_____

_____

4. This Psalm outlines David's frustration with evildoers who delight in wickedness. David finds comfort in the truth that evildoers will soon fade away. If the desires of your heart are at war and your anxiety about unfulfilled yearnings is rising, check the source and longevity. Are your desires centered on self, or on God? Are they short-lived, or will they last for the long run? Use the chart below to evaluate unmet desires in your heart:

Desire	Spirit-surrendered or self-centered	Immediate gratification or eternal satisfaction

5. David encourages the readers to "commit your way to the Lord; trust in him, and he will act. He will bring forth your righteousness as the light, and your justice as the noonday" (Psalm 37:5-6). If your desires are for things to be made right, this is in alignment with God's heart. Write a prayer to commit your way to God and put your cares in His hands:

_____

_____

_____

6. It may look like those who follow their heart and realize their desires through unjust means are successful. David said something about this too: "Be still before the Lord and wait patiently for him; fret not yourself over the one who prospers in his way, over the man who carries out evil devices!" (Psalm 37:7). Who are you elevating more than the Lord? Release this person to the merciful hands of God:

_____

_____

_____

_____

7. "Refrain from anger, and forsake wrath! Fret not yourself; it tends only to evil" (Psalm 37:8). David was hunted by his father-in-law but resisted the opportunity to murder his pursuer. His closest officers ridiculed him for not taking the chance to seize the throne. He refrained. He knew that worry led to evil— he was steadfast and waited for God's timing. Is there something you're tempted to take instead of being steady and waiting?

_____

_____

_____

_____

_____

Put your hand on your heart and find your heartbeat. If you are sitting and calm, this is likely your resting heart rate. Notice during the day when your heart quickens of its own accord. We often register emotion in our bodies before we can name the feeling in our minds. A faster heart rate means your body is preparing you for movement, whether in excitement or fear. When you notice your heart beat, make that a time to ask God to give you the desires of His heart, and let your hearts beat as one.

Write a prayer based on today's reflections:

_____

_____

_____

_____

Now that you have written your prayer, step away from external images and tune in to the Lord in centering prayer. Keep your hand over your heart as you practice aligning yourself with the peace of His presence.

Day 5: Let's Review

Prompt: When you feel pulled apart in every direction, remember who you are.

Promise: *"Now this is what the Lord says—He who created you, O Jacob, and He who formed you, O Israel: 'Do not fear, for I have redeemed you; I have called you by your name; you are Mine!'"* — *Isaiah 43:1*, BSB

Recap + Quick Quotes:

This week, we uncovered the messages that pull us apart from God's peace. With Scripture as our lens, we redefined the messages from culture that tell us to be true to ourselves, to do it all, that we are enough, and to follow our heart. Instead of chasing our identity elsewhere, we are reminded to return to God's promises for peace.

- "Being 'true to you' as a Christian means being true to the person you already are in Christ. Being true to you is walking by faith in God's presence."
- "But doing more than what God's will prescribes divides us and separates us from the peace we have in Christ."
- "On the cross, Jesus said, 'it is finished.' Isn't this enough? Let your anxiety rest at the foot of the cross. Let this be the holy ground from which you stand."
- "The sinful heart set on survival is loud, desperate, and resistant to change. But the mind set on the spirit is life and peace."

Group Discussion Questions:

a. *Main question:* What's one thing that has clicked with you and God this week? How have you experienced His peace in light of this week's study?

b. *Day 1:* What feelings does the phrase "be true to you" bring up?

c. *Day 2:* Have you felt the pressure to do everything? What contributes to that feeling—family background, being a parent, digital media, or something else?

d. *Day 3:* What would it mean for you to "make it your ambition to live a quiet life"?

e. *Day 4:* David knew that worry led to evil, and but he was steadfast and waited for God's timing. Is there something you're tempted to take instead of being steady and waiting?

f. *Bonus question:* What is the main thing that divides your mind and separates you from God's peace? How can you put it aside in favor for a whole-hearted devotion?

Prayer:

Lord,
You prayed for us to be one with You, as You are with the Father. May we not stand in Your way. May we not let the distractions of our day or the messages of culture muddy our minds and lead our hearts astray. You have redeemed us, formed us, called us by name. May we hear You calling us by name and sit with Your voice over our hearts for the next two minutes. We come to you now. [Let two minutes pass.] Amen.

Group Prayer Requests

_____

_____

_____

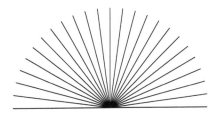

Session 2: Redefining Perfect Peace

When we continue to hear the deep gentle voice that blesses us, we can walk through life with a stable sense of well-being and true belonging.

Henri J. M. Nouwen[4]

---

[4] Henri J. M. Nouwen, *Life of the Beloved: Spiritual Living in a Secular World* (New York: The Crossroad Publishing Company, 1992), 73.

Day 1: Peace Starts with God

I had no reason to be at peace: I was about to go into labor! But as God suggested in that moment, I didn't do a whole lot to make the baby grow. I loved my husband, I ate food, I slept, and the baby miraculously grew into a human being. Pregnancy was much bigger than me. "Life starts with God," I reckoned. "And if God began this baby, He will bring the baby through," I concluded. But still, the possibilities of what could go wrong abounded. I could read all the books, make all the birth plans, and do all the coaching classes, but nothing would guarantee a healthy, happy baby and mama. The fact that we cannot control outcomes is most striking in a birthing situation but applies to all of life. Peace, therefore, is not a result we can achieve, but a state we may return to.

But try as we may, we still try and create this state of being through hard work and preparation. But a peaceful dove will not land on a restless, rushing heart. Even when the baby comes, when the diapers need to be changed, when work piles up, when we get overwhelmed by our own limits, it's not enough to achieve lasting peace. We simply cannot maintain it. And therein lies the secret: we can't...but God can. And He has. Instead of running to seize up peace in preparations, may we be like Jesus coming out of the waters of baptism, humbly receiving the Spirit.

Thankfully, the Spirit was already preparing my heart before birth. A friend sent me a very special verse that I stored in my soul. You can store it up too: "You keep him in perfect peace whose mind is stayed on you, because he trusts in you" (Isaiah 26:3). Peace, thank God, is not found in abilities or perfect outcomes, but remains in the centering presence of God. As Max Lucado says, "the path to peace is paved with prayer."[5] When a situation or responsibility feels too big to handle, start with God. Pray. When anxiety pulls your thoughts astray and you don't know where to go, start with the very first word of this verse: "*You...*" Let the humility of this simple prayer help you come back home to the peace of the Lord. Life starts with God, and so does His peace. Start with this promise, and you'll always start on the right track.

"You keep him in perfect peace whose mind is stayed on you, because he trusts in you." —Isaiah 26:3

Write the verse below, and underline the words that speak to your heart today:

_____

_____

_____

1. What do you do to find peace in your life? Is it accomplishing a to-do list, taking medications, doing meditations? Do those lead to the lasting peace you need? Explain.

_____

_____

[5] Max Lucado, *Anxious for Nothing: Finding Calm in a Chaotic World* (Nashville: HarperCollins, 2017), 87.

_____

_____

_____

2. Notice the verse above starts with God. How does this comfort you when you feel like all the pressure is on you to create and keep the peace?

_____

_____

_____

_____

3. Isaiah 26:3 describes the peace God offers as "perfect peace." The word "perfect" here means *completeness* or *wholeness*. What is your definition of "perfect," and how does it compare with God's definition?

_____

_____

_____

_____

4. What is our role in Isaiah 26:3? What does this mean to you?

_____

_____

_____

_____

5. Think of a conflict in your life, whether it's within you or another area you need peace. According to your previous answer, what is your role in creating peace within the conflict?

_____

_____

_____

_____

6. Our ability to trust is based on past faithfulness. What has God done for you in other situations that will allow you to put your trust in Him now?

_____

_____

_____

7. What thoughts keep you from putting your trust in God alone? Let go of thoughts that do not belong to a person whose peace is in the Lord. Write them here for clarity:

Ways I trust in myself:	How I can trust God instead:

Oxford Language Dictionary defines peace as "a state or period in which there is no war or a war has ended." Your heart doesn't always feel at peace because your feet are on earth where the battle for souls is still raging. Theologian Meister Eckhart does not define peace as an absence of wars, but instead says: "in Christ equals peace." Christ won the war, and when our minds are stayed on Him, God will keep us in His perfect peace, no matter what is happening in your life. Anytime you are tempted to despair of the hopelessness of trying to achieve peace, pause. Make intentional space for God. Let Him keep you in His perfect peace.

Write a prayer below and confess where you are not at peace. Allow the spirit to remind you that you are, by faith, in Christ:

_____

_____

_____

_____

Spend some time in centering prayer. Take a word or symbol from your prayer above and hold it in your heart, being with God and letting Him align you with His peace.

Day 2: Redefining Perfect

During the end of one very long Christmas break, I was at the end of my rope. I stomped up the stairs with gritted teeth to find my girls yelling at each other and playing tug-of-war with a stuffed kitty in a room that looked like a toy bomb went off. My face flushed with anger. The room was chaotic, the kids were misbehaving, and I was on the verge of deforming into monster mom. I was fixated on the imperfections, which is all I could see. If only we could achieve perfection, we would find the peace we are looking for, right?

Aiming for perfection itself ends in the disease of perfectionism with symptoms like short-sightedness, failure, and despair at the expense of inner peace. We often say things like, "progress over perfect" to console ourselves from our shortcomings and protect our ego. Deficiency is pride's enemy. But inwardly, we like things to be perfect. We crave perfection. And the Bible doesn't condemn perfection. In fact, Jesus says, "You therefore must be perfect, as your heavenly Father is perfect" (Matthew 5:48). But how?

When I looked for imperfections, I found them. But when we look to Christ, we find perfection. In the light of His glory, we can see the world rightly through the lens of grace and redemption. We can rest from our own efforts because Jesus has finished the work of salvation. All there's left to do is patiently allow God's work to play out. God defines perfection as the process of spiritual maturity to make us complete *in Him* through the sufferings of Christ.

Before I completely lost it, the Lord stopped me dead in the center of my girls' room and said, "Look at them. They are Mine, and so are you. You're angry because you can't control everything. What I want is for you to be free to enjoy your family, even this room...to enjoy Me." I melted. I had lost sight of the Lord. When rooms are disordered and so is life, start with God and get aligned with the perfect peace He gives now. Things may not look beautiful on the outside, but He is working *all things* together for the purpose of salvation. He promises to complete (or perfect) the work He starts in us, and sometimes uses messy rooms to achieve His purposes. His ways are perfect. You can trust Him.

"You, therefore, will be perfect [growing into spiritual maturity both in mind and character, actively integrating godly values into your daily life], as your heavenly Father is perfect." —Matthew 5:48, AMP

Write this version of Matthew 5:48 below:

_____

_____

_____

1. When have you felt dismayed by reaching for perfection? What was your reaction when you fell short?

_____

_____

_____

_____

2. What was your idea of "perfect" at the time? Was it an image, an idea, or something else? Describe what you had hoped for.

_____

_____

_____

3. Consider the verse "you must be perfect, as your heavenly Father is perfect" as explained in the Amplified translation. Does this version change your perspective of perfection? What do you notice?

_____

_____

_____

4. Contrast God's idea of perfection from Matthew 5:48 to your picture of perfection from question one. What do you think He wanted you to see and be in that moment?

_____

_____

5. Do we need to be perfect right now? How does "growing into spiritual maturity both in mind and character" allow each moment to be a place of training rather than a pass or fail test?

_____

_____

_____

_____

6. The Amplified Bible version speaks about "actively integrating godly values into your daily life." This suggests that each opportunity is not a way to prove ourselves, but rather to discern and define who we are in Christ with our actions. Instead of needing everything to work out the way you expected, how can you focus on each small decision? How do you want every decision reflect and align with your values?

_____

_____

_____

_____

_____

7. You *will* be perfect, as your heavenly Father is perfect. This verse doesn't mean we must become perfect on our own, but gives us a view of our Father's intentions for us. He allows each trial and temptation to form us to the image of Christ. Look once more at your explanation from question one. How can you see this situation through God's eyes as a way to perfect and align you with His design for your formation?

_____

_____

_____

_____

_____

_____

The Greek word for "perfect" in this verse is *teleios*. HELPS Word-studies says: "The root (*tel-*) means 'reaching the end (*aim*).' It is well-illustrated with the old pirate's telescope, unfolding (extending out) one stage at a time to function at full-strength (capacity effectiveness)."[6] If you have a telescope, pull it out for a real-life illustration. If not, just imagine your life as a telescope partly extended. You can see, but not yet the whole picture. As time unfolds like a telescope, you will have a more accurate perspective of the events in your life. Our view may be

---

[6] Strong's Greek: 5046. τέλειος (TELEIOS). Accessed March 20, 2023. https://biblehub.com/greek/5046.htm

imperfect now, but trust that God can see the whole picture, and He has a plan for perfection. You are living in it right now. Rest in the peace of His purposes and perfect will for you today.

Write out a prayer based on today's reflections:

_____

_____

_____

_____

Exhale and unfold yourself into a pose of surrender. As an art connoisseur would know the difference between a fake painting and a real one, ask the Creator to show you what the real meaning of perfect is before you let other images convince you. Spend time in centering prayer on the word "perfect," allowing all other images to fade away.

Day 3: Peace is Always with You

"I'm scared," my daughter said, biting her lip as she peered out the car window at the kids flooding into camp. "It's okay to be scared," I reassured her. "You know what? I've heard that courage is fear that has said its prayers." I proceeded to sing a rousing performance of "I've Got Peace Like a River" before she cut me off with an embarrassed look. I was mostly singing that for myself anyway. *Did I bring everything she needs? Would she be okay by herself?*

In the Bible, the Greek word for worry combines the verb *divide* with the noun mind. Worry divides the mind.

Max Lucado explains more in his book, *Anxious for Nothing*: "Worry takes a meat cleaver to our thoughts, energy, and focus. Anxiety chops up our attention. It sends our awareness in a dozen directions."[7] When we worry, we completely forget that God's perfect peace is always with us. Peace is not dependent on circumstances; it cannot be lost in the shuffle of the crowd. Peace cannot be compromised by your performance.

Like perfection, if peace can be lost, it's not truly real. Both peace and perfection lie in the unshakable, eternal place of God's presence. Peace, like the Lord, is always there at the still center of our soul, waiting for us.

How can we make a point to consistently return to that peace

---

[7] Lucado, Anxious for Nothing, 148.

like a river in our soul? Psalm 94:19 says, "When the cares of my heart are many, your consolations cheer my soul." God's comfort renews our hope, brings us joy, and soothes our divided hearts. When worry scatters our attention, the peace of God draws us back and makes us whole. When my daughter returned to me at the end of her day at camp, she was smiling. And so was I. I believe God smiles every time we return to Him, too. No matter what new situation awaits or what fears surround you, know that God's perfect peace awaits you. Peace is always with you in the presence of God. You're welcome back, truly, anytime.

"When the cares of my heart are many, your consolations cheer my soul." —Psalm 94:19

Put on some worship music as you write down the verse below:

_____

_____

_____

1. What do you have a hard time holding on to? Are you absent-minded, forgetful, or do you sometimes want to freeze time to capture a precious moment?

_____

_____

_____

2. Do you believe God's peace is always with you? When is it hardest to believe this truth?

_____

_____

_____

_____

3. Different translations of Psalm 94:19 say "when doubts filled my mind" (NLT) or refer to "the multitude of...thoughts" (KJV) crowding our heads. For highly sensitive people, too much stimulation at one time causes emotional flooding. Do you have too many stressors in your life right now? Write down the common denominators in your anxious episodes:

_____

_____

_____

4. Max Lucado compared worry to a meat cleaver dividing the mind, chopping up our awareness. Is this an accurate description for you, or does a different image come to mind? Explain.

_____

_____

_____

_____

_____

5. Another Psalmist prays, "unite my heart to fear your name" (Psalm 86:11). Elsewhere, it is Jewish tradition to recite, "The Lord our God, the Lord is one" (Deuteronomy 6:4). Later in Exodus, the first commandment teaches us to fear God and Him alone. How is the Lord's design for us to be aligned with Him different than the enemy's tactics to divide and conquer through worry? Can you name a time that staying close to the Lord provided peace? How is this moment different than anxiety?

_____

_____

_____

_____

6. Psalm 94:19 proclaims that God's "consolations" cheer us. Like a piece of stray metal to a strong magnet, a single word of the Lord can pull us together. Name a Scripture or phrase from our verse that can bring good news to the cares of your heart:

_____

_____

_____

7. If God keeps in perfect peace those whose minds are stayed on Him, then how can you use your mind to stay in His peace?

_____

_____

_____

_____

Just as Satan made Eve doubt God in the garden, he still uses causes confusion today. Worry makes us feel like we have lost our peace, but the Word reminds us it is already ours in Christ. Today when you are tempted to worry, ask yourself, "What do I already have in Christ? What promises has He given me? What have I not asked for that He says He will give to me?"

Write a prayer:

_____

_____

_____

_____

I can recount many times when God's faithfulness has provided comfort when I was consumed by worry. In a moment of centering prayer, ask God to show you all the riches you have in Christ, as in Philippians 4:19: "And my God will supply every need of yours according to his riches in glory in Christ Jesus." You can repeat a breath prayer on the inhale: "In Christ," and on the exhale "I have _____." Keep repeating until you feel at peace.

Day 4: Returning to Life

For cattle ranchers, fencing is not only expensive, but requires constant vigilance. In places like Australia where the living conditions are harsh and the land is broad, there is no need for fencing. The cattle stay close to the watering hole because they know what brings life. Anxiety divides the mind, scatters our senses, and splits up our strength. The best way to get realigned with peace as our center is not to put more rules up like fences to keep anxiety out, but to come back to God's peace like a watering hole for a thirsty soul.

We can apply this analogy to a life of peace with God. Living as God's loved ones in a hostile world can feel callous and unforgiving. But once we taste the peace that comes from Christ, we will keep coming back for more. Returning to God's perfect peace requires awareness of our desperate state, like a parched tongue that can only be satisfied with living water.

One such thirsty soul was the woman at the well from the Gospel of John. As she and Jesus conversed, it became apparent she was caught up in the rules of worship that fenced her out from a relationship with God. It was clear she wanted a better solution than to keep coming to that well. Jesus encouraged the woman to ask Him for living water: "Everyone who drinks of this water will be thirsty again, but whoever drinks of the water that I will give him will never be thirsty again. The water that I will give him will become in him a spring of water welling up to eternal life" (John 4:13-14). She was not fenced out, she was invited in. The first one, in fact, that Jesus openly reveals Himself to.

Jesus shows Himself to us in the Word. His living presence is like an underground spring, right underneath our very feet, the source of all hope and life. We can put up fences and excuses for not going to God. We can use food, Netflix, or good company to grant temporary peace. But Jesus says we need to ask for better. We need to ask Him for life and peace. Jesus is the truest, purest, most steady source of peace we will ever find in this life. If you are on the fence right now, position yourself around the well of life. Come back to the river of eternal life and peace, and stay close. This is your official invitation.

"The water that I will give him will become in him a spring of water welling up to eternal life." —John 4:14

Write down the verse, replacing the word "him" with your own name as if Jesus was directly addressing you:

_____

_____

1. Read the full story of the woman at the well in John 4. She was tired of drawing water from the well. Viewed as a social pariah, she went to the well in the heat of the day to avoid other women. She wanted Jesus to give her the water that didn't run out so she wouldn't have to keep suffering in this way. What are you tired of doing? What are you hoping will finally bring you peace?

_____

_____

_____

_____

2. John 4:14 says, "Everyone who drinks of this water will be thirsty again." What earthly, non-renewable sources of peace do you rely on?

_____

_____

_____

_____

3. Anxiety reigns when chaos escapes outside of our manmade fences. What would it feel like to know you no longer had to depend on controlling a situation, but could depend on your near and present God in the moment? What fences may you be using as an excuse to keep you from God?

_____

_____

_____

_____

4. Jesus told the woman: "The water that I will give him will become in him a spring of water welling up to eternal life."

Have you asked for this living water, the relief that comes from God alone? If you have not, take a moment to ask Jesus for His living water. Be assured that Jesus promised in John 6:35, "whoever believes in me shall never thirst." Believe, and ask in confidence.

5. After receiving the words of Jesus and believing Him to be the Messiah, the One who could meet all her needs, the woman left her jar of water at the well. What could you release so God can send you His gospel peace? Perhaps it's a destructive habit that no longer serves you, a relationship that draws you away from the Lord, or a mindset that doesn't align with the peace of God.

_____

_____

_____

_____

6. Springs of water come from underground. Instead of continuing to draw water from an external source, how is the Spirit of God an accessible hidden resource? In what area of your life are you only living on the surface, but know God has more for you? How will you reach out to dig deeper?

_____

_____

_____

7. The world promises temporary fixes, but Jesus offers more. We are forever people and He wants to provide the peace we need not just in this life, but always! How does this generosity of the Lord give you peace regarding your dilemma from question one?

_____

_____

_____

_____

The next time you get up to do something, whether going to the pantry out of hunger, putting on a sweatshirt for comfort, or going on a walk to leave behind anxiety, consider its ability to give you what you need. Give thanks to Jesus that He meets your greatest need even when everything else is stripped away. And when you do receive, know that "every good gift and every perfect gift is from above" (James 1:17). Thanking God for each moment of provision is like returning to the wellspring of life. The woman at the well turned around and told everyone she knew what God had done for her. Consider how even saying a simple table blessing out loud can grant others the peace of God with us, meeting every need.

Write a prayer from today's time together:

_____

_____

Instead of trying to center the world around your needs, try centering yourself in the presence of God, in the middle of His living streams of water. Let His goodness rush over you as you hold a word of hope in your heart, like a rock in a riverbed, smoothed by the steady flow of grace.

Day 5: Let's Review

Prompt: Remind yourself that perfect peace starts with God.

Promise: *"You keep him in perfect peace whose mind is stayed on you, because he trusts in you"* —Isaiah 26:3

Recap + Quick Quotes:

This week, we defined the perfect peace that Jesus gives so we can search for it as our heart's home base, the center of our soul's alignment. We established that peace doesn't start with us, but with God. We redefined our role in perfection, were comforted to know that peace is always with us, and saw our craving for peace as a natural solution to a seeking heart.

- "Peace starts not in what we can do, but with who He always is."
- "Instead of wanting things to *be* perfect, let us instead find peace in *the One* who is perfect. Then, we will find perfect peace."
- "Like perfection, if peace can be lost, it's not truly real yet. Both peace and perfection lie in the unshakable, eternal place of God's presence."
- "Returning to God's perfect peace is being fully aware of our desperate state, like a parched tongue that can only be satisfied with living water."

Group Discussion Questions:

a. *Main question:* What's one thing that has clicked with you and God this week? How have you experienced His peace in light of this week's study?

b. *Day 1:* Where do you find peace in your life? Is it accomplishing a to-do list, taking medications, doing meditations? Do those lead to the lasting peace you need? Explain.

c. *Day 2:* Do we need to be perfect right now? How does "growing into spiritual maturity both in mind and character" allow each moment to be a place of training rather than a pass or fail test?

d. *Day 3:* How is the Lord's design for us to abide in Him different from the enemy's tactics to divide and conquer through worry? Can you name a time that staying close to the Lord provided peace? How does this moment compare?

e. *Day 4:* In what area of your life are you only living on the surface, but know God has more for you? How will you reach out to dig deeper?

f. *Bonus question:* How does perfectionism harm your mindset? How can God's perfect peace guard your heart and mind in Christ?

Prayer:

Lord,
Forgive us for looking to ourselves to control our circumstances and for getting frustrated when we can't make things perfect. Replace our disease of perfectionism with prayer and the perfect peace to

endure through every situation. Then we will see that You are perfect and You are redeeming all things—including us. Sometimes that plan means we have to go through suffering, but we know You are victorious, and in You, we have peace. We rest our hearts in Your ways for the next two minutes. We come to you now. [Let two minutes pass.] Amen.

Group Prayer Requests

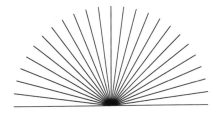

Session 3: The Path to Realignment

Intuition is seeing with the soul.
— Dean Koontz

Day 1: Willingness to Feel

As she sat on the couch sharing about her difficult college roommate, I noticed her shoulders slumped and felt her emotional heaviness. Even after I prayed for her, it seemed she hadn't heard me at all—she couldn't see the hope I saw for her future. She was closed off, weighed down with anxiety. It hurt me, too. How could I get through to her, lift her up, encourage her? As a highly sensitive person, I can relate to others who suffer with anxiety. Hyper-aware of our surroundings, we often absorb the pain of others and feel overburdened.

We are bombarded daily with messages from our environment, people, and media. Our peace depends on discernment from a place of soul safety. Did you know that we have nine times as many afferent signals to our bodies than internal ones? That means the number of messages your nervous system receives is far greater than the messages your body sends. The onslaught of incoming messages crushes us when we let them accumulate. Spiritually, Proverbs 12:25 describes anxiety as heaviness: "Anxiety in a man's heart weighs him down." But the verse doesn't end here—and neither does your anxiety. The "but" implies there is another way, that we don't have to be yoked with anxiety. The rest of the verse says, "but a good word makes him glad."

The first step to realignment with God's peace is the good word of the gospel. God Himself keeps you in perfect peace. Know that you are safe with Him, that nobody can take away your salvation, and your future is secure with Jesus. From this refuge, you can tune in to your physical sensations when you feel unsettled in your spirit. Not being okay is your sign to come back to God and consult with Him. If we notice signs of anxiety, if we feel our heart racing, our head aching, or mind wandering, may we discern what is from God and what is not. What is part of God's peace, and what is pulling us out of alignment? It may take a friend to look you in the eye, lift your head and say, "Hey, that sounds hard." Sometimes we just need someone in it with us to release us from ourselves and bring us back to God's peace. Anxiety weighs us down, but a good word lifts us up. May the Good Word lift you up today.

"Anxiety in a man's heart weighs him down, but a good word makes him glad." —Proverbs 12:25

Feel the position of your head and shoulders. Are they collapsed forward? Roll your shoulders back, lift the crown of your head, open your heart, and write the verse below:

_____

_____

_____

1. Signs of anxiety may include but are not limited to:

   - A sense of tension, apprehension, or dread
   - Disconnection with reality
   - Insomnia
   - Panic attacks
   - Fatigue
   - Headaches
   - Inability to concentrate

These are mental and physical signs of anxiety, but you may also feel uneasiness, distraction, and fixation on despairing outcomes. This exercise is not meant to diagnose an anxiety disorder, but simply to help you recognize early symptoms (please see resources in the Appendix for more help). Begin the process of awareness by underlining the feelings you can relate to above, and write down any others you experience as a lack of peace:

_____

_____

_____

2. Anxiety can be due to genetics or generational tendencies that you can't always control. Anxiety can stem from unresolved, buried trauma. Anxiety can also be triggered by everyday stimulants and stressors. Think of a time when you felt heavy with anxiety. What do you believe contributed to your feelings of anxiety? Is there anything you can do to be aware of, prepare for, and manage these triggers?

_____

_____

_____

3. The New American Bible says, "Worry weighs down the heart," and the Douay-Rheims Bible says, "Grief in the heart of a man shall bring him low." The words "weigh down" also means "to bow down in homage." When fear gets stuck in our hearts, it

brings us low, takes us away from the worship of God, and turns us in on ourselves. How do you believe God longs to comfort you while you are in this state?

_____

_____

_____

4. The Good News Translation of Proverbs 12:25 says, "Worry can rob you of happiness, but kind words will cheer you up." When you feel robbed of happiness, how have your circumstances affected the condition of your heart? How is God's steadfast, unwavering presence a comfort to you?

_____

_____

_____

5. Who has given you a good word in a time of anxiety and changed your sorrow into the joy and confidence of hope, even if just for a time? What did they say that spoke peace to your heart?

_____

_____

_____

6. A compassionate and encouraging word can give someone relief, comfort, and restore their peace with God: "The Lord God has given me the tongue of those who are taught, that I may know how to sustain with a word him who is weary. Morning by morning he awakens; he awakens my ear to hear as those who are taught" (Isaiah 50:4). May we open our ears to allow God to teach us words to lift up the anxious in heart. Who can you lift up, and with what good words? Take action and send the message to them now.

_____

_____

_____

7. Proverbs 14:10 says, "The heart knows its own bitterness, and no stranger shares its joy." While we can do our best to encourage others, peace ultimately comes down to a personal relationship with Jesus Christ. What anxious thoughts would you like to exchange for God's good word? You may refer to the promises of God in the Appendix.

Anxious thoughts	Good Word

You don't have to allow anxious thoughts to lodge in your heart. Reset your posture, and become the gatekeeper of your thoughts. Allow your identity in Christ to be like a cat at a mousehole—wait and see what thought comes out next. Practice this with the following exercise from *Holy Noticing*: "As thoughts rise up in your mind, try to reframe troublesome ones such as *I am anxious* to a decentered thought such as *I am having feelings of anxiety*, which provokes less anxiety. By labeling thoughts this way, you're adding some distance between them and their effects on you."[8]

Write a prayer based of today's reflections:

_____

_____

_____

_____

    Spend a moment in silence, stillness, and centering prayer with the Lord.

---

[8] Stone, *Holy Noticing*, 160.

Day 2: From Scattered to Centered

Chin bent over the steering wheel like a crazed Cruella De Vil, I raced to my daughter's school. My heart pounded as I berated myself for being late. I could see her disappointed face etched into my mind from the last time I cut it close for pickup. "I was the *last one!*" I was just trying to tie up a few things for work at home, and even left the sink a dirty mess as I snatched my snoring three-year-old from her bed and buckled her in. *But wasn't being on time more important than a few emails?* My priorities were scattered, and my anxiety skyrocketed.

The demands of life can pull us off course from our core values. One sign we are deviating from the Lord's path for us is anxiety: racing pulse, doom and gloom thoughts, feelings of helplessness and hopelessness. The thought, "I should have left earlier," can quickly snowball into shame: "I'm such a bad mom." These surface-level problems devolve into identity pigeonholes. If I had that level of guilt regarding a school pickup, can you imagine how Jesus' disciples must have felt after abandoning him before the cross?

But even Jesus' very best friends left, and he did not condemn them. Rather, he comforts them. He comforts you. In John 16:32-33, he told his disciples: "You will be scattered...and will leave me alone...I have said these things to you, that in me you may have peace. In the world you will have tribulation. But take heart; I have overcome the world." Jesus was hurt deeply. But He did not wallow in self-pity. He knew there was a bigger truth. This world does have trouble. There are kids to pick up, clothes to be folded, trauma to work through, and rent to be paid. But when you're scattered, here's your consolation: we may be in a world of trouble, but there is always more peace in the Word. When I finally arrived at the school pickup line, the teachers were picking up the cones. I frantically waved out the window, and they sent my daughter out. To my surprise, none of the teachers had a scowl on their face. They were glad I was there, and phew, so was I. The consequences for being scattered is not a reprimand, but a reminder to return to what truly matters. And even when we do fail (He knows we will), take heart: Jesus has already overcome. We can rest in Him.

"I have said these things to you, that in me you may have peace. In the world you will have tribulation. But take heart; I have overcome the world." —John 16:33

Look away from the mess around you. Close your eyes and lift your head to the heavens. Take a deep breath as if you are taking in the peace of heaven, and as you exhale and open your eyes, return God's peace to the space you are in. Write the verse below:

_____

_____

1. Some signs of being scattered for me include a messy living space, being late, and feeling anxious. What are your signs of scatteredness? What are your feelings?

_____

_____

_____

_____

2. What is your baseline, or your state of peace? We can only have a sense of what's right if we have already been there. We can only be homesick for heaven if we've come from God Himself. What does being at peace mean to you? Describe it below:

_____

_____

_____

3. I sacrificed being on time to finish up work, and let my daughter down. But being there for her was more important to me than a few emails. I learned the work of relationships is worth the result of peace. What important area of your life is suffering at the expense of less important, tertiary matters? Name three areas of your life that, when they are aligned, you feel generally at peace:

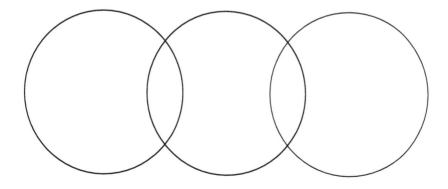

4. In order to understand John 16:33, we must backtrack and see what "things" Jesus said to his disciples. John 16:32 says: "Behold, the hour is coming, indeed it has come, when you will be scattered, each to his own home, and will leave me alone. Yet I am not alone, for the Father is with me." When you are scattered and anxious, have you considered that your actions reflect the disciples' fear, leaving Jesus and scattering from Him? Tell him about that:

_____

_____

_____

Be comforted that Jesus knew He was never alone, and He desires the same for you.

5. In what or whom does Jesus say you will have peace? Note that this is a promise of God.

_____

_____

_____

_____

6. Jesus tells us the truth: we will have tribulation. You will still feel sorrow and experience trouble, but this does not nullify God's Word. Instead, He encourages us to take heart, have courage, and cultivate joy. The Amplified Bible explains

Jesus' statement: "I have overcome the world" with [My conquest is accomplished, My victory abiding.] Your life might feel scattered, but don't worry, this is normal. His full victory is yet to come, but you can take heart in Him right now. What troubles did Jesus have, and what is the peace He lives in right now?

_____

_____

_____

_____

7. How are you able to share in both Jesus' sufferings and in His peace?

_____

_____

_____

_____

How do you sharpen a knife? You run it through a sharpener, which has wheels on either side to bring the stray edges of the knife back to the center. Pastor Cleddie Keith said, "A knife cuts because it has a narrow focus." When anxiety separates our heart from God's joyful purpose, we need to get sharpened. Take action today to sharpen the focus on one of the important areas of your life you identified on question three.

Write a prayer based on today's reflections:

_____

_____

_____

_____

When you're scattered, your attention is on the world rather than in the Word. Let go of the anxiety that comes with unending trouble, and marinate in the peace of God's victory with centering prayer.

Day 3: Growing in Maturity

For every inch your head is held forward out of neutral alignment, you add an additional ten pounds of weight to your spine. But I didn't care about that. I was nursing my last baby, and getting to witness her satisfaction after getting her fill of milk was something I wasn't going to miss. Once she was full, she would stretch her elbows out wide, arch her back, make a little duck face with her mouth, and promptly fall asleep. Every time. It delighted me to no end. My back sorely needed physical therapy after that, but it was worth it. Unfortunately, pain-free doesn't guarantee being peace-filled—that's the joy of sacrifice we learn as we give our life away to others in love. The complete maturity to which God calls us has less to do with growing up independently and more about growing upright in Christ, together.

We may stop physically growing, but we always aim to mature. And as we get older, we must fight invisible forces stay upright. Being out of alignment causes pain, which signals us to get back in line. Once we are functionally stacked along the plumbline of gravity, proper alignment and peace is generally restored. The key to good alignment is not just a strong spine, but a balance of tension. Tensegrity is a term that explains the balance of tension and compression that creates stability. First, there's the compression of our spine being properly stacked upright. This is synonymous to our desires being in alignment with upward calling of Christ. The tension of our limbs that pull outwardly mirrors the healthy relationship with a body of believers. These two forces working together create integrity within our design and allow us to walk forward.

When my neck and back were tense while breastfeeding, it's because their job was to hold onto my head so it didn't fall off. Tension is good. If you're experiencing pain or tension in your life, consider these messages a cue to come back to the body, to the center of stability in Christ with others. Under the authority of Christ, we are properly aligned with God and able to nourish and cherish one another as Jesus does for us. Ephesians explains further: "Until we all attain to the unity of the faith and of the knowledge of the Son of God, to mature manhood, to the measure of the stature of the fullness of Christ" (Ephesians 4:13). Maturity is your calling in Christ. Keep growing in alignment with Him.

"Until we all attain to the unity of the faith and of the knowledge of the Son of God, to mature manhood, to the measure of the stature of the fullness of Christ." —Ephesians 4:13

Write down half of the verse below until the word "God," asking someone else in your home or friend group to write down the other half:

_____

_____

_____

_____

1. Take a moment to be still. Where do you feel the most tension in your body? Put a hand on that spot, send some compassionate breaths toward the tension, thanking God both for the ability to hold on so long and also for the grace

to let go and get back into alignment. Jot down a professional who might be able to help you release that chronic tension, like a local chiropractor, massage therapist, or physical therapist. Consider other areas of your life where you feel tension, and view that tension as a call to unity to come back to the center. Write down those areas of tension below:

_____

_____

_____

_____

2. Our goal is to attain to the maturity of Christ "so that we may no longer be children, tossed to and fro by the waves and carried about by every wind of doctrine, by human cunning, by craftiness in deceitful schemes" (Ephesians 4:14). When we lean into the wisdom of God and all the saints, we stave off the anxiety of being battered by the changing tides of culture. We can stand firm. Where are you weary from trying to stand strong against a trendy teaching disguised as truth?

_____

_____

_____

_____

3. "Until we all attain to the unity…" suggests that maturing in Christ is not an individual endeavor but a group effort. We are truly stronger together. Where is the "unity of the Spirit in the bond of peace" (Ephesians 4:3) lacking in the church? Name some examples where you do see this unity:

_____

_____

_____

_____

4. Read Ephesians 4:1-13. What does it mean to grow in spiritual maturity? What verse resonates with you most and why?

_____

_____

_____

_____

_____

5. Let's dig into Ephesians 4:13. The word "knowledge" here means "knowledge gained through first-hand relationship."[9] Alignment is putting knowledge into

---

[9] "Recognition, Knowledge," Strong's greek: 1922. Accessed March 20, 2023. https://biblehub.com/greek/1922.htm

practice. How are you growing in your personal, experiential relationship with Jesus? Name the ways:

_____

_____

_____

_____

6. When it feels like you don't know your place in the body of Christ, consider your spiritual gifts. Ephesians 4 outlines the spiritual gifts that Jesus gives us to "equip the saints for ministry, for building up the body of Christ" (Ephesians 4:12).

    A) Circle a spiritual gift from Ephesians 4 that speaks to you:
        Apostle: special representative
        Prophet: speaks messages from God to people
        Evangelist: spreads the good news
        Shepherd: guides the people in God's ways
        Teacher: instructs from God's Word

    B) How can you exercise your spiritual gift to build up the body of believers?

_____

_____

_____

_____

7. Consider that Jesus is more invested in our spiritual growth than we are. Since we are part of His body by faith, our growth is His growth. Our pain is His pain. He not only takes care of the church, his body, but promises to carry on to completion the good work he started in you (Philippians 1:6). What have you been taking charge of that can you release to His authority today?

_____

_____

_____

_____

This work will not be done in a day, but is a labor of constant love that starts with Christ. Illustrate this by resetting your alignment, starting with your head. Whether standing or sitting, slide your chin back so your ears rest directly over your shoulders. Open your hands to roll your shoulders back, rest your ribcage over your hips, and back up your hips until they sit directly over your heels. Once everything is stacked correctly, the members of your body don't have to work so hard. From proper alignment, you can function from a place of peace.

Write a prayer based on today's reflections:

_____

_____

_____

Take a word from your prayer above or Ephesians 4:13 and spend a few moments in centering prayer, allowing the Lord to steadily grow you in spiritual maturity until the day of Christ Jesus.

Day 4: Walking in Integrity

Three years into her naturopathic doctoral degree, Megan owed $120,000 in student loans, and she was ready to walk away. It no longer felt right. She didn't want to base her patient outcomes on pleasing insurance companies or overwhelm patients with complicated treatment plans. Having tuned in to her core values, Megan felt like she didn't align with this program anymore. And yet her degree was almost finished. Should she continue down a path she didn't agree with, or give it up and find a new path, carrying a massive amount of debt with her?

At certain crossroads in life, walking away with integrity is worth more than the cost to continue down a trajectory we know is not right. Integrity is moral soundness, and walking in integrity is doing what we believe in accordance with the truth. The Bible rarely talks about integrity alone, and usually pairs it with the action of walking. Walking not only gets us places, but strengthens us as we go.

This week, we talked about what it feels like to be off-center. One sign of anxiety is uneasiness in everyday situations. Paul told his disciple Timothy about how to be aligned with God's peace: "The purpose of my instruction is that all believers would be filled with love that comes from a pure heart, a clear conscience, and genuine faith" (1 Timothy 1:5, NLT). As Coach Taylor from the show *Friday Night Lights* would say: "Clear eyes, full heart, can't lose." Clouds of doubt and insecurity have no place in the fullness of God's sure love. When we are filled with the love of His spirit, He will guide our steps, and send up red flags when we are out of step with His peace. Integrity is listening in obedience and walking in the knowledge of God by grace.

So which path did Megan choose? She chose integrity. After graduating, she established a naturopathic coaching practice to help others. She gives them assurance of heart, clarity of mind, and the courage to walk in the integrity of what is right for their health and healing. She can do this because the love of God leads the way. We may not be able to see the whole path, but we can follow the Lord into the next right step.

"The purpose of my instruction is that all believers would be filled with love that comes from a pure heart, a clear conscience, and genuine faith." —1 Timothy 1:5

Write the verse down below, underlining the characteristics of love that stick out to you:

_____

_____

_____

_____

1. What big or small situation are you currently uncertain about?

_____

_____

_____

_____

2. What do you believe is the right thing to do, and how can you trust God with the cost of doing it?

_____

_____

_____

_____

3. Paul tells Timothy that his hope is for all believers to be filled with love. How can God's love fill and guide you in the situation you described in your answer from the first question?

_____

_____

_____

_____

4. Paul's warning in the previous verses is to: "charge certain persons not to teach any different doctrine, nor to devote themselves to myths and endless genealogies, which promote speculations rather than the stewardship from God that is by

faith" (1 Timothy 1:3-4). When we focus on speculation and all the what-ifs, our locus of control—the belief in our ability to change our life—is external. When we put stewardship into action, we strengthen our integrity and exercise God-given agency. In the circle below, write what you do know and can do. Outside of the circle, write the doubts and unknowns. Focus on what you can do inside of the circle, and pray about the rest.

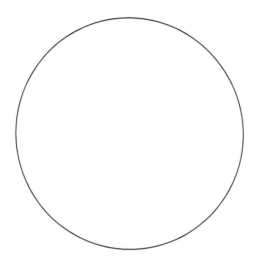

5. Paul wants us to be filled with love that comes from a pure heart, which is set on delighting itself in the Lord with no hidden motives. Know that God loves to hear from you. Lay your heart bare before Him and tell Him what you earnestly desire, but struggle with. These are feelings and hopes you do know. You may use Psalm 32 and Psalm 119:9 as a guide.

_____

_____

_____

6. The second character quality is a clear conscience. A clear conscience does not mean we are guiltless but rather living unashamedly before the face of God. What part of your life are you holding back from the Lord? Know that in Christ there is no room for condemnation; only invitation for confession, repentance, and sanctification.

_____

_____

_____

_____

7. The last quality of this solid love is genuine faith. Sincere, unfeigned faith is not just word and talk but deed and truth (1 John 3:18), not just faith without works but showing our faith by our works (James 2:18). The real proof of our faith is how it plays out in our life. When do your words and actions not line up with your faith, and what causes you to stray? You may need to backtrack through the last two questions and assess your conscience, and then ask God to search your heart for any anxious ways.

_____

_____

_____

_____

Go on a prayer walk today. Designate one foot to symbolize righteousness, and the other peace to reflect Psalm 85:10. As you walk, notice how they balance each other and move you forward at the same time. Thank God for His love for you, and ask Him to grant you a pure heart, clear conscience, and genuine faith when it comes to the crossroads you are working through. Trust that He will lead you in what is right, "and the effect of righteousness will be peace, and the result of righteousness, quietness and trust forever" (Isaiah 32:17). May we walk in the integrity of our hearts before our gracious God today.

Write a prayer based on today's reflections here:

_____

_____

_____

_____

Now take a word from your prayer above for a few moments before the Lord, and keep returning to this word to strengthen your center in Him.

Day 5: Let's Review

Prompt: Identify the steps to realignment with the Lord.

Promise: *"I have said these things to you, that in me you may have peace. In the world you will have tribulation. But take heart; I have overcome the world."* —John 16:33

Recap + Quick Quotes:

This week, we discussed walking the path to realignment with God's peace. We start with noticing when emotions feel heavy and we expect to carry the load. Then we identify which areas of our life feel inconsistent with what we believe is important. We reach out to others in line with the kingdom's vision to grow in peace together, and then walk the path with integrity.

- "If we can gently notice small signs of anxiety, we can begin to discern what is from God and what is not. May this verse be a simple guide: anxiety weighs you down, but a good word lifts you up."
- "But when you're scattered, here's your consolation: we are in a world of trouble, but there is peace in the Word."
- "Pain-free doesn't guarantee being peace-filled—that's the joy of sacrifice we get to learn as we give our life away to others in love."
- "Integrity looks like listening in obedience and walking in the knowledge of God by grace."

Group Discussion Questions:

a. *Main question:* What's one thing that has clicked with you and God this week? How have you experienced His peace in light of this week's study?

b. *Day 1:* Who has given you a good word in a time of anxiety and changed your sorrow into the joy and confidence of hope, even if just for a time? What did they say that spoke peace to your heart?

c. *Day 2:* What important area of your life is suffering at the expense of less important, tertiary matters? Name three areas of your life that must be aligned for you to feel at peace.

d. *Day 3:* Ephesians 4 outlines the spiritual gifts that Jesus gives each one of us to "equip the saints for ministry, for building up the body of Christ" (Ephesians 4:12).
   i. Circle a spiritual gift from Ephesians 4 that speaks to you:
      1. Apostle: special representative
      2. Prophet: speaks messages from God to people
      3. Evangelist: spreads the good news
      4. Shepherd: guides the people in God's ways
      5. Teacher: instructs from God's Word
   ii. How can you exercise your spiritual gift to build up the body of believers?

e. *Day 4:* What area of your life are you on the fence about? What do you believe is the right thing to do, and how can you trust God with the cost of doing it, no matter what happens?

f. *Bonus question:* How do you know the right thing to do in any given situation?

Prayer:

Lord,

We don't want to go the wrong way. We know that You hold eternal life, so where else could we go? Keep us sensitive to Your spirit, keep us aware when we go astray, and lead us back to your path of peace. Your ways are good, true, and right. We trust you to always lead us back to You. For the next two minutes, we ask You to search our heart and show us what is out of alignment with Your will for us according to Your word. We come to you now. [Let two minutes pass.] Amen.

Group Prayer Requests

_____

_____

_____

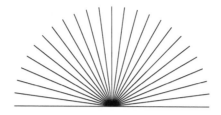

Session 4: Name What You Do Not Know

We see not as things are but as we are.

—Brené Brown

Day 1: Alligators Under the Bed

Raise your hand if you've ever pole vaulted into your bed to escape the imaginary alligator lurking below? I recently witnessed my little girl jumping a little too quickly into her bed, and I wonder how many adults still worry about someone or something grabbing our ankles if we stand too close. We've all heard stories of gremlins, alligators, or burglars waiting for us under there. But even worse, my husband actually hid under the bed and jumped out at my six-year-old one night. No wonder she's terrified! Darkness is a symbol of the unknown. Our questioning mind fills in the blanks with a menagerie of possibilities. This is why kids develop a fear of the dark–their minds make up scenarios to complete the picture, no matter how unrealistic it might be.

The same goes with anxiety. Anxiety is labeled as a general and undefined sense of tension, apprehension, or dread. I am reminded of Psalm 53:5, which portrays those who do not know the Lord as those "in great terror, where there is no terror!" Left to our anxiety-ridden devices, we often imagine the worst-case scenario. Part of this is a survival mechanism, but much of the narratives we entertain are not only unhealthy but simply untrue, misaligned with the goodness of God and the care He has for His children.

The challenge is to internalize what we know to be true, and consciously, deliberately, let go of what we don't. We must be vigilant to lean into the wisdom of Deuteronomy 29:29, which says: "The secret things belong to the Lord our God, but the things that are revealed belong to us and to our children forever, that we may do all the words of this law." Once we discern the difference between what knowledge belongs to us and what belongs to the Lord, we can let go of unnecessary anxiety. We can live peacefully within the boundaries of our God-given domain, and trust Him with everything else that is His to reign. We may even be able to casually step into our beds at night, Lord willing.

"The secret things belong to the Lord our God, but the things that are revealed belong to us and to our children forever, that we may do all the words of this law." —Deuteronomy 29:29

Write down the verse below. Then, erase the words "secret things," and note how you feel with those words gone. Write them back once you finish the questions below.

_____

_____

_____

_____

1. When we face the unknown, we worry like Mark Twain: "I've had a lot of worries in my life, most of which never happened." What were you most scared of as a kid that has yet to happen to you?

_____

_____

_____

_____

_____

_____

_____

2. We might not worry about alligators under the bed anymore, but there are other fears: break-ins, shootings, sickness and more. What fears are you convinced will happen to you?

_____

_____

_____

_____

3. Consider Deuteronomy 29:29 from above. "The secret things belong to the Lord our God" refers to the counsels, plans, and future purposes God has in store for us. Matthew Henry's commentary says, "He has kept back nothing that is profitable for us, but only that of which it is good for us to be ignorant."[10] As God told us not to eat of the tree of the knowledge of good and evil, some things are best left

_____

[10] Matthew Henry, "Matthew Henry's Concise Commentary," Deuteronomy 29:29, Commentaries (Bible Hub). Accessed January 13, 2023. https://biblehub.com/commentaries/deuteronomy/29-29.htm.

untouched and unknown. Do you ever feel like God is holding back from you? How?

_____

_____

_____

_____

4. Do you trust God to tell you what you need to know and ask Him for answers when you don't? Why is this difficult to do? See James 1:5 for assurance.

_____

_____

_____

_____

5. The middle of Deuteronomy 29:29 says, "the things that are revealed belong to us and to our children forever." These "things" at the time of Deuteronomy referred to the law of God as given by Moses. Now, we even have the full revelation of God in the person of Jesus. Ephesians 1:9-10 says God was, "making known to us the mystery of his will, according to his purpose, which he set forth in Christ as a plan for the fullness of time, to unite all things in him, things in heaven and things on earth." How has Jesus already told

you what you need to know in the midst of the unknown? Write it here:

_____

_____

_____

_____

6. The last section of Deuteronomy 29:29 says that what God has revealed to us belongs to us so that "we may do all the words of this law." God gives us the law because it is good and right and holy, and has our best in mind. But the history of the Bible shows that we cannot follow the law. We cannot stay within the boundaries of His peace by our own works. So we are comforted by 1 John 5:3-4: "For this is the love of God, that we keep his commandments. And his commandments are not burdensome. For everyone who has been born of God overcomes the world. And this is the victory that has overcome the world—our faith." We live not by works but by faith in the Living Word, who is Christ. How does resting in His presence as the fulfillment of the law enable us to be humbly obedient?

_____

_____

_____

_____

7. We do not know all things, nor do we need to know all
    things. But we can know what God has given us in His Word.
    Think of something you are worried about. How can God's
    Word comfort you? Write down a verse that speaks to you,
    or underline the following promise: "Fear not, for I am with
    you; be not dismayed, for I am your God; I will strengthen
    you, I will help you, I will uphold you with my righteous right
    hand" (Isaiah 41:10).

_____

_____

_____

_____

_____

_____

Put yourself in a dark room where you can't see a thing. What fears creep into your mind about the unknowns in the room? Bugs crawling on the wall? Scared you will bump your head? Be still for a moment, and feel the ground under your feet and the air in your lungs. Use your given senses to the utmost. The floor represents the foundation of what God has revealed to us and breath signifies the Spirit of God with us. Even when it feels like we are floundering in a foreign land of what-ifs, God gave us His Word to stand firm. He gave us Jesus to be with us. May we use all of our senses to be with Him, too.

Write a prayer from today's reflections:

_____

_____

_____

_____

During a moment of centering prayer, let God transform any worries into the beauty of His mysteries by centering in on His Son.

Day 2: How to Rule the World

How can a good God allow suffering? This is an age-old question that Job learned the hard way. His perplexing story from the Old Testament shows how Job endured loss of family, scorn of friends, and scourge of his health. His own wife became an enemy to him and accused, "Do you still hold fast your integrity? Curse God and die" (Job 2:9). *Harsh.* Yet Job remained faithful: "For I know that my Redeemer lives, and at the last he will stand upon the earth" (Job 19:25). Job refused to renounce the two things he knew for sure: he was suffering, and God would redeem Him.

To Job's amazement, God appeared in response to prayer, but he did not explain why Job was suffering. God did not mention Satan demanding to test Job's devotion to God. Instead, God took Job on a tour of the earth to demonstrate how He runs the world every moment for all eternity. He showed off all the creatures He created and cares for, from the birds of the air to dangerous beasts. The experience left Job with the humbling conclusion that God would take care of him, too.

Job's story is comforting. Even though we don't know why bad things happen, or how we will cope when we are in need, God takes care of us. And just as God visited Job to show Him how He rules and reigns, He came to us in the form of His only Son, Jesus. And again, God stood upon the earth and pointed to the animals to calm our worried hearts. In His Sermon on the Mount, Jesus said, "Look at the birds of the air: they neither sow nor reap nor gather into barns, and yet your heavenly Father feeds them. Are you not of more value than they? And which of you by being anxious can add a single hour to his span of life?" (Matthew 6:26-27). We are worried, but He is not.

God has been taking care of business since the beginning of time. Not knowing how God will provide for us is scary, but Job's story and Jesus' illustration remind us that we don't have to rule the world. That's God's job. Our role is simply to let the peace of Christ rule in our hearts. From there, as God's own sons and daughters, we can partner with the Almighty in taking care of the earth in all its wild and wonderful ways.

"Look at the birds of the air: they neither sow nor reap nor gather into barns, and yet your heavenly Father feeds them. Are you not of more value than they? And which of you by being anxious can add a single hour to his span of life?" —Matthew 6:26-27

Write down "look at the birds of the air," then, if you're by a window, look outside and see if you can spot any birds, people or pets. Consider how God is taking care of each of them from beginning to end. Continue writing the verse, contemplating this for your own life.

_____

_____

_____

_____

1. We live our life forwards, but often understand it backwards. Do you have any situations in your life that felt

devastating at the time, but now you can see how God has redeemed it for good? Explain.

_____

_____

_____

_____

2. Do you have any unresolved periods of suffering? Does it affect your attitude about God's ability and affections toward you? If so, how?

_____

_____

_____

_____

3. Jesus' first direction is to lift our eyes to the sky. He said, "Look at the birds of the air." How often does anxiety cause us to look down? How does looking up help us see how we are part of the world God is in charge of?

_____

_____

_____

_____

_____

4. Jesus then said, "they neither sow nor reap nor gather into barns, and yet your heavenly Father feeds them." I used to think this verse meant the birds didn't have to work for their food. But considering the phrase, "the early bird gets the worm," I see that birds aren't just waiting for somebody to drop food in their mouth (adult birds, anyway). They look underground for the worms God has provided, even though they can't see them. What are you worried about, and how can God give you eyes to seek what He has hidden for you?

_____

_____

_____

_____

5. "Are you not of more value than they?" This does not mean we are superior to birds, but that God cares for us as His children, made in His very image. You are precious to Him because you are a part of Him. Imagine Jesus delivering this verse to you. Do you believe Him? Explain.

_____

_____

_____

6. "And which of you by being anxious can add a single hour to his span of life?" I imagine Jesus asking this to a crowd, and everyone looking around to see if any hands are raised. Nobody? So why does being late heighten anxiety? We think we will run out of time. So we rush around like maniacs, and push and prod everyone else to do the same. But worry has no power over time. Only God does. Time is in His hands, and so are you. Think of how worry is directly related to time in your day. How can you trust God with His timeline as a means of provision for you?

_____

_____

_____

_____

7. Most of our worry revolves around what we cannot control. But Jesus comforts and reminds us that God is taking care of every single thing. Instead of worrying about how to run the world, let His peace rule in your own heart: "And let the peace of Christ rule in your hearts, to which indeed you were called in one body. And be thankful" (Colossians 3:15). Which feels more aligned with God's will: world domination, or letting God's peace rule your heart?

_____

_____

_____

Jesus delivered his sermon from Matthew 6 outdoors. When we open the door, we step outside of ourselves, too. We enter into God's creation plan in action, plants and animals thriving in an intricate ecosystem of His design and constant care. Make some time today to go outside and observe all that God cares for, starting with the smallest of details: how ants build a home one grain of sand at a time, how a leaf is shaped to take in sunlight and funnel rain to its roots. The workings of nature are quiet reminders of God's majestic qualification as King, and give us faith that He is also working out the details of our own lives.

Take a moment and write a prayer from today's reflections:

_____

_____

_____

_____

Corrie Ten Boom said, "Never be afraid to trust an unknown future to a known God." Take a few moments of centering prayer to be in the presence of the Lord, to know Him and be known.

Day 3: Not Knowing When

There I was, in the middle of a dead-end job while I waited for my future husband to propose. Not that I was just waiting on him, mind you. My mom always raised me to be an independent woman, and the Bible taught me that the best waiters serve. I was trying to make the most of my job in the middle of a recession, but I was in Georgia and the love of my life was in Seattle. I think I asked him every two weeks if this relationship was "going somewhere" (read: "When, approximately, will you ask me to marry you?") He would say, "Just trust me," but I still wanted a timeframe. I liked to plan out my life, and not knowing *when* was seriously frustrating. Waiting is so hard, right? Even when you do trust God, not knowing *when* is the most difficult part of living by faith.

When it comes to waiting, I can relate to Sarah from the Bible. When she was sixty-five years old, well past child-bearing age, God promised her a son. She laughed. It was impossible! But the seed of hope had been planted. When she still wasn't pregnant after eleven years, Sarah and Abraham took matters into their own hands and had a son through her servant. But no amount of time or human interventions can keep God from fulfilling His promises. After twenty-five years of waiting, Sarah birthed Isaac, a direct ancestor of Jesus. What God says He will do, He will do. We don't always know *when* He will fulfill His promises, but we can find peace in knowing that He *will*.

After three years of dating, the seed of hope was planted in me, too. I wanted to start a life together with my best friend. Little did my anxious self know, my future husband was working out a marriage proposal. We got married, had our first daughter on Valentine's Day six years after our first date, and named our second daughter Sara. This verse hangs on her wall to remind us who to trust: "By faith Sarah herself received power to conceive, even when she was past the age, since she considered him faithful who had promised" (Hebrews 11:11). She is a living reminder of God's faithfulness. God promises peace, no matter what, no matter when. Let us give thanks for how He proves Himself over and over, and align ourselves in trust while we wait for every single one of His promises to be fulfilled.

*"By faith Sarah herself received power to conceive, even when she was past the age, **since she considered him faithful who had promised.**" —Hebrews 11:11*

Write down the bolded part of the Scripture above:

_____

_____

1. When have you been so impatient with one of God's promises that you tried to do it yourself? Biblical examples include Sarah from Genesis 16:2 and King Saul from 1 Samuel 13:8-14.

_____

_____

_____

2. When have you waited on God, what did He do that you couldn't?

_____

_____

_____

3. What are you still waiting on?

_____

_____

_____

4. Hebrews 11 is considered the "hall of faith" and lists those who acted in response to God's promises to them. Many of them did not receive what they were waiting for in this life. But Hebrews says they saw the promise from afar and greeted it as their own, and "therefore God is not ashamed to be called their God, for He has prepared for them a city" (Hebrews 11:16). Do not be ashamed of hoping for what you do not yet have. If God has planted a promise in your heart based on His Word, be sure you will receive it in His timing. God promised Sarah she would have a son. What do you hope for that may not be what God has promised? What has God promised you that you can be sure He will do? See promises in the Appendix and write down one below you need help believing:

_____

_____

_____

_____

5. One promise God made to Jesus was that He would be King.
    Jesus did not take the throne before God's timing, did not
    yield to Satan in the desert (Matthew 4:9), did not listen to
    Peter when he opposed him about the crucifixion (Matthew
    16:23). He was obedient unto death. And God kept His
    promise. What kind of opposition do you experience
    waiting for God's promises in your life? Do others doubt
    what God has told you? How can the example of Jesus
    encourage you when it's hard to wait?

_____

_____

_____

_____

6. Just as my husband was working out how to provide for us
    before He proposed, God is often working things out in the
    background of our lives. In Daniel 10:12-14, Daniel fasted and
    mourned for three weeks. An angel arrived and explained
    the delay: he had been fighting other demon angels while
    Daniel waited for God's response. Also consider Elisha from
    2 Kings 6:17, who saw heaven's armies fighting for his
    people, when his servant did not. We do not know how God
    is fighting for us right this very moment. Hebrews 7:25 says
    that Jesus "always lives to make intercession for [those who
    draw near to God through Him]." How does this knowledge

comfort you regarding your answer from question three? What other things may God work out in the waiting?

_____

_____

_____

_____

7. The author of Hebrews said "faith is the assurance of things hoped for, the conviction of things not seen" (Hebrews 11:1). As Matthew Henry's Concise Commentary says, "Faith can lay hold of blessings at a great distance."[11] Which of God's promises can you consider as good as done, even if you don't see complete fulfillment in this life? How does this change your perspective of the future?

_____

_____

_____

_____

Timing is not always ours to know. Even Jesus said he did not know when the Day of the Lord would be (Matthew 24:36). Another translation of Hebrews 11:11b says, "She rested the

_____

[11] Matthew Henry, "Matthew Henry's Concise Commentary," Hebrews 11:11 Commentaries (Bible Hub), accessed January 1, 2023, https://biblehub.com/commentaries/hebrews/11-11.htm.

authority of her faith on the One who made the promise." Rest your faith not in timetables, but in the person and power of God. The next time you are tempted to fret over the calendar or check your phone for a notification, take it as your cue to go to the Lord instead. Ask Him for answers first. Head to the Appendix for what He says will happen for sure. I trust you will find the reassurance you need for today.

Write a prayer based on today's reflections:

_____

_____

_____

_____

Spend some time in centering prayer, repeating the phrase to the Lord in worship: "You are faithful."

Day 4: What You Look For, You Will Find

We never truly know what other people are thinking. We don't know the suffering in their story. And if we did, we would have a whole lot more compassion for one another. I used to be intimidated by my backyard neighbor, and the house she had flipped from *yuck to yuppie* had me thinking, "She is way out of my league!" Then she came to my 6 a.m. neighborhood boot camp class during the pandemic and she's now the first one I call for advice. I later found out she spent many lonely months as a new neighbor, praying for some good friends. *Why hadn't I reached out earlier?!*

We don't know what others are going through because we each live in the dark recesses of our own minds. Ephesians says: "They are darkened in their understanding, alienated from the life of God because of the ignorance that is in them, due to their hardness of heart" (Ephesians 4:18). We often concoct false assumptions about the world and each other based on innate negativity biases, giving more attention to unfavorable possibilities.[12] Negativity bias prepares us for threats, but living in defense mode is exhausting. But there's another bias working in our favor, and that's confirmation bias. What you look for, you will find. Where your focus goes, energy flows. When we believe this is our Father's world, we will look for Him and find his works.

---

[12] Cacioppo JT, Cacioppo S, Gollan JK. The negativity bias: Conceptualization, quantification, and individual differences. *Behavioral and Brain Sciences.* 2014;37(3):309-310. doi:10.1017/s0140525x13002537

By the light of Christ, we can see clearly! And the light has come: "For God, who said, "Let light shine out of darkness," has shone in our hearts to give the light of the knowledge of the glory of God in the face of Jesus Christ." (2 Corinthians 4:6). As we turn away from the shadows and toward His light, we can dwell in peace as God's people. Even in the darkness, we are all in this together under one Son. We can look for the shadows and confirm our fears, or we can look for the light. And we will find it (1 Chronicles 22:19). And who knows? We just might find a new best friend in the girl next door.

"For God, who said, 'Let light shine out of darkness,' has shone in our hearts to give the light of the knowledge of the glory of God in the face of Jesus Christ." —2 Corinthians 4:6

Find a light source nearby, whether that be a candle, window, or lamp, and let it illuminate your paper as you write down the verse. Underline "in the face of Jesus Christ":

_____

_____

1. Have you ever assumed the worst about somebody and were later proven wrong? Share what you learned and how that changed your perspective:

_____

_____

_____

2. What feels scary in the world right now?

_____

_____

_____

_____

3. Living in the shadows puts our focus on the unknown. Does this ever feel safer than being exposed to the light of truth? How does anxiety protect you? How does it harm you?

_____

_____

_____

_____

4. What do you believe causes you harm? Perhaps you believe that somebody dislikes you, or that you'll never find the right job, or that you'll always struggle with anxiety?

_____

_____

_____

_____

5. The same God who created the sun created you. If He can light up the whole world every day, He can shine light into your darkness, too. Name a time when you were struggling in the darkness of fear and God said, "let there be light," and changed your entire perspective. Share how different you were before and after:

_____

_____

_____

_____

6. Light is not just what we see, but through which we see everything else. Light helps us see truth, and here's the truth: God so loved the world that He came to save us (John 3:16), He considers us sons and daughters of great worth (2 Corinthians 6:18), and Jesus will be with us always (Matthew 28:20). God is light, but He isn't just a beam of electrons. The light, the glory rays, emanate from the face of Christ. He is the only source of all light. Take your answer from the last question and bring it before the face of Jesus. You can say something like, "Jesus, I believe _____, but You say _____."

_____

_____

_____

_____

7. God relates to us face-to-face. Are you afraid of someone in your life who you need to confront or connect with? Remember that we do not fight against flesh and blood, but against the spiritual forces of evil in the heavenly places (Ephesians 6:12). Consider that it is not the person you are afraid of, but the forces of darkness. But light does not fear the darkness, nor is it anxious about the future. It simply shines. As you consider how to go forth in this relationship, ask God's light to go before you.

We may not be plants, but we still benefit from the healing properties of sunshine. Bright morning light is shown to be effective against insomnia, painful menstrual cycles, and seasonal affective disorder. Sunlight also helps produce serotonin, which makes us feel happy and calm.[13] Get out in the sun today and enjoy the free gift that is God's light, aligning yourself with God's peace in this promise: "The light shines in the darkness, and the darkness can never extinguish it" (John 1:5, NLT).

---

[13] Mead, M Nathaniel. "Benefits of Sunlight: A Bright Spot for Human Health." Environmental health perspectives. U.S. National Library of Medicine, April 2008. https://www.ncbi.nlm.nih.gov/pmc/articles/PMC2290997/#:~:text=The%20melat onin%20rhythm%20phase%20advancement,affected%20by%20exposure%20to% 20daylight.

Write a prayer based on today's reflections:

_____

_____

_____

_____

For centering prayer today, let your spirit focus on the face of the Son.

Day 5: Let's Review

Prompt: Name what you do not know. Bring up these questions in prayer to the Lord and be held in the mystery.

Promise: *"The secret things belong to the Lord our God, but the things that are revealed belong to us and to our children forever, that we may do all the words of this law."* —Deuteronomy 29:29

Recap + Quick Quotes:

This week, we put a name to what we do not know. For anxiety, we name it to tame it. We did the work of discerning between what we need to know, and letting the unknown belong to the Lord. Like Job, we do not know how to rule the world, but we can let peace rule our hearts. Like Sarah, we may not know when God will do what He says, but we can trust Him. And as we wait in the unknown, we look for the light of reality.

- "Once we can discern the difference between what knowledge belongs to us and what belongs to the Lord, we can let go of unnecessary anxiety. We can live peacefully within the boundaries of what He wants us to steward, and trust Him with everything else that is only His to reign over."
- "Job's story gives us comfort in this: even though we don't know why bad things happen, or how we will cope when we are in need, God is taking care of us."

- "We don't always know when He will fulfill His promises, but we can find peace in knowing that He *will*."
- "As we turn away from the shadows and toward His light, we can dwell in peace as God's people. Even in the darkness, we are all in this together under one Son."

Group Discussion Questions:

a. *Main question:* What's one thing that has clicked with you and God this week? How have you experienced His peace in light of this week's study?

b. *Day 1:* What were you most scared of as a kid that has yet to happen to you?

c. *Day 2:* How can you trust God with His timeline as a means of provision for you?

d. *Day 3:* What are you hoping for that may not be what God has promised? What has God promised that you can be sure He will do?

e. *Day 4:* Name a time when you were struggling in the darkness of fear and God said, "let there be light," and changed your entire perspective. Share how different you were before and after:

f. *Bonus question:* What does focusing on what you know versus what is unknown do to your mental health?

Prayer:

Lord,

Even though we act like it, we don't know everything. And that's a good thing. We submit to you what we do not know, and trust You. You are a good and kind ruler, and our life is in your hands. We open our hands in a posture of surrender, and as we close our eyes, we acknowledge that even darkness is light to You. You never leave us alone. Shine your light into the darkness, starting in our own hearts. We come to you now to bask in Your presence for the next few minutes. [Let two minutes pass.] Amen.

Group Prayer Requests

_____

_____

_____

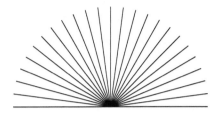

Session 5: Live What You Know

"This cup, this cup I wanna drink it up. To be right here in the middle of it...This challenging reality is better than fear or fantasy." *This Cup* by Sara Groves

Day 1: God Is with You—Where Are You?

The unmistakable wail of a tornado siren pierced the silent eerie sky, and terror struck my heart. Wherever my mind had been wandering until that point, I was quickly pulled back to reality. I knew by instinct and preparation what I needed to gather and where I needed to go, but I also wrestled with worry: "Was my husband okay where he was traveling? Would I have enough phone power or service to call for help if needed? How long would this last?" But time was of the essence. I realized I could spend time worrying about what could happen, or I could run to safety. Emergencies tend to snap us back to reality and align us with the hard truth of the present. We can worry, or we can run.

When disaster strikes, where do we go for safety? Do we worry about the what-ifs, or run to what we know? I'd love to say we always go to a trustworthy place, but the truth is, we go to where we've been before. We go straight to what feels familiar. It's so important to not only have an emergency plan, but to practice it—to go through the motions and ingrain the muscle memory so the path there becomes second nature. When we go into survival mode, we can't always access the most sensible parts of our brain, but we do act on trained impulses.

Let us evaluate our emergency worry plan: what is familiar for us now, and what can we trust? How can we align what we trust with where we go? Psalm 46:1 says "God is our refuge and strength, a very present help in trouble." Immanuel, God with us, is accessible in proximity and presence. If we don't automatically go to God as a trusted familiar place, we can start today. Every time we go to Him, we lay down a neuropathway, making it easier for our brain to take that way again.

I rehearsed going to the tornado shelter under my house and prepared what I'd bring with me. In a similar way, we can repeatedly go to God. Some ways to practice becoming wholly present with God is to posture our bodies in kind: kneeling when we need to ask God for help, putting our hands together in an act of unity, standing in reverent awe before Him. But as you practice turning away from worry and running to the real refuge in Christ, you just might find that what started out as emergency worry drills have become your place of peace.

"God is our refuge and strength, a very present help in trouble" — *Psalm 46:1*

Write today's promise below, pausing for two seconds in between words:

_____

_____

_____

1. When an emergency shakes you to your core, you need firm ground to stand upon. You need solid answers. Let's evaluate your unshakeable beliefs here. What do you know for sure?

_____

_____

_____

_____

2. In her book, *The Way of Integrity*, Martha Beck follows up
   this question with another: how can you be absolutely sure?
   The second question helps debunk any false narratives you
   might hold about what you believe and reinforces what is
   true. Write with this prayer as your filter: "Search me, O
   God, and know my heart! Try me and know my thoughts!
   And see if there be any grievous way in me, and lead me in
   the way everlasting" (Psalm 139:23-24).

_____

_____

_____

What forms the foundation of your answer? Past experience,
present knowledge, the confirmation of others, your faith?

_____

_____

_____

_____

_____

3. We change, but God does not. He allows us to experience refinement, lead us to Himself, and leaves only what is good and true. What did you used to believe with absolute certainty that God has since changed your mind about?

    _____

    _____

    _____

4. Do you have a hard time being mindful in the moment? If so, what pulls you away from the present? What helps you stay grounded?

    _____

    _____

5. The whole of Psalm 46 is beautiful. Read it now, and consider the Psalmist's conclusion in verse one. Even if the worst happens, we will not fear. Even if, let's say, "the earth gives way...the mountains be moved into the heart of the sea," (Psalm 46:2), we will not fear. Sometimes we need to let our fears play out to see the folly. Even if the worst comes true, the greatest good is still true: God is still our refuge and strength during the storm. What is the worst possible thing you fear right now, and how can God be your refuge?

    _____

    _____

    _____

6. Later in Psalm 46, the Psalmist says: "The nations rage, the kingdoms totter; he utters his voice, the earth melts," (Psalm 46:6), which seems like a legitimate cause for worry. Even when the present is difficult, how can we exalt the Lord? Underline the relevant phrases in Psalm 46:10-11: "Be still and know that I am God...I will be exalted among the nations, I will be exalted in the earth!' The Lord of hosts is with us; the God of Jacob is our fortress. Selah." How can a heart posture of peace exalt the Lord in your situation?

_____

_____

_____

_____

7. God is a "very present help in trouble," or "always ready to help in times of trouble" (NLT). When you are anxious, are you aware that God is ready and willing to help you the moment you call on Him? What prevents you from asking for help when you are worried?

_____

_____

_____

_____

_____

Do you know what always lives in the present even when our minds wander? Our bodies. Getting back into our bodies will help integrate our mind and settle our spirit. One stress-relieving way to do this use the 5-4-3-2-1 sensory exercise. You can do this right where you are. Describe five things you see, four things you hear, three things you feel, two things you smell, and one thing you taste. Let the future melt away as you focus only on your surroundings. Take a deep breath, prayerfully saying, "I am here. God, you are here with me." May this exercise connect you with the peace God offers in His presence, who is with you everywhere you go.

Write a prayer based on today's reflections.

_____

_____

_____

_____

During centering prayer, release the *what-ifs* with each exhale, and focus on the Rock *that is* with the inhale: God with you in the moment, present and ready to help.

Day 2: You Have God's Approval

I stood in front of the watching audience, a foot taller and twenty years older than my fellow violin students. My heart was thumping and I was nervous—which I felt embarrassed about—I was an adult in a kid's recital! And then came the applause. Why was everyone clapping? I hadn't even started! Growing up playing sports, I learned you don't start with the crowd's approval: you win it. But this was different. My violin teacher explained that in concerts, the audience shows their support at the beginning. I could get on board with that. How much more could we start our day with peace if we knew we started out with God's approval?

Think about how often we wake up with the anxious thought: "So much to do, so little time!" and rush around like the work of the world rests on our shoulders. But on the cross, Jesus said, "It is finished." The work of salvation is done. This is what theologians would call living in the era of "already." Our faith starts here. But the reality of sin and suffering shows that God has not yet finished the work of redemption. This is called the future "not yet." Bible commentator Nicky Gumbel describes the three tenses of salvation: "You have been saved from the penalty of sin. You will be saved from the presence of sin. You are being saved from the power of sin."[14] Being aligned with this spiritual timeline means living in the middle: giving thanks for what God has *already* done in the past, walking with God now, resting in calm assurance for the *not yet.*

---

[14] Gumbel, Nicky. Bible in One Year 2020 with Nicky Gumbel. You Version. Accessed January 4, 2023. https://www.bible.com/ur/reading-plans/17704-bible-in-one-year-2020-with-nicky-gumbel/day/145#!

The promise here for us is this: "Therefore, since we have been justified by faith, we have peace with God through our Lord Jesus Christ" (Romans 5:1). The best daily reminder you can integrate into your life is what you believe when you wake up in the morning. Do you work for the peace of rest, or do you work from the peace of rest? God isn't asking you to show-off, only to show up—He already has. God approves of you, beloved. May His face shining on you be your peace today.

"Therefore, since we have been justified by faith, we have peace with God through our Lord Jesus Christ." —Romans 5:1

Instead of writing God's promise below, write the above verse on a scrap of paper and set it on your bedside so you can see it when you wake up first thing in the morning.

1. Do you believe you already have God's approval? Why or why not?

_____

_____

_____

2. When have you had to work for approval? Do you think that experience feeds into your idea of how God views you?

_____

_____

_____

_____

3. Whenever we see the word "therefore" we should ask,
    "What is the 'therefore' there for?" If we backtrack to
    Romans 4, Paul explains how the promise of God rests on
    faith, and calls to mind the example of Abraham. Slow down
    by tracing your finger along the words so you don't miss a
    word meant for you:

    > No unbelief made him waver concerning the promise of
    > God, but he grew strong in his faith as he gave glory to
    > God, fully convinced that God was able to do what he
    > had promised. That is why his faith was 'counted to him
    > as righteousness.' But the words 'it was counted to him'
    > were not written for his sake alone, but for ours also. It
    > will be counted to us who believe in him who raised
    > from the dead Jesus our Lord, who was delivered up for
    > our trespasses and raised for our justification. (Romans
    > 4:20-25)

Underline what sticks out to you in the verses above. Where are
you not fully convinced that God is able to fulfill all His
promises? What doubts get in the way?

_____

_____

_____

_____

4. Romans 5:1 says, "we have been justified by faith." Notice that this is past tense. The New Living Translation says, "we have been made right in God's sight by faith." We are acquitted from sin, the gavel has fallen in our favor, we are declared blameless in God's sight. This can be hard to believe because we still sin. How are we blameless—by our ability not to sin, or something else? What does this verse say we are justified by, and how does this change your heart in what you do?

_____

_____

_____

_____

5. The next part of the verse says, "we have peace with God through our Lord Jesus Christ." Imagine playing at a music recital before the judge of the universe. Now imagine playing as a child for a kind Father. Because of Jesus, you too are God's child, and He loves you. He's going to sing with you, give you a standing ovation with overflowing love in His eyes. His words confirm this: "he will rejoice over you with gladness; he will quiet you by his love; he will exult over you with loud singing" (Zephaniah 3:17). Do you start your day basking in His love, or miss Him by rushing around, trying to prove yourself?

_____

_____

_____

6. God the Father vocalizes His affirmation of Jesus before Jesus even starts His official ministry. As He is raised from the waters of baptism, Matthew records that "a voice from heaven said, 'This is my beloved Son, with whom I am well pleased'" (Matthew 3:17). Baptism is a public profession that we now live by faith, not by works. What is your experience with baptism, and what is your hope for it?

_____

_____

_____

_____

_____

7. Another remembrance of God's love for us is communion. Jesus says in Luke 22:19: "And he took bread, and when he had given thanks, he broke it and gave it to them, saying, 'This is my body, which is given for you. Do this in remembrance of me.'" Our sin came at a great cost, and Jesus was willing to pay it. Taking communion reminds us that Jesus gave us everything: his body, his life. How can your body and the way you live your life be a living sacrifice today (Romans 12:1)? What act of love feels costly, but possible thanks to the gratitude you feel for how Jesus has given Himself for you?

_____

_____

_____

_____

_____

What mementos of God's faithfulness as a remind you of what God has done for you? Here are a few ideas to surround yourself with His love:

- Write God's blessings on stones and stack them in a garden or shelf.
- Put up a chalkboard of thankfulness where you record what God has done for you each day.
- Next to pictures on a shelf, on a wall, or across a banner, add Scripture like, "Great is your faithfulness" (Lamentations 3:23).

Pick an idea from above, or choose your own way to remember God's faithfulness. I will remember God's faithfulness today by

_____

_____

Spend a moment in centering prayer focusing on the phrase, "peace through Jesus."

Day 3: Better than We Can Imagine

As we sat on the couch cradling our hot cinnamon spice tea, I invited my college friend to reflect before she embarked on her career. "Now that you're about to graduate, what would you go back and tell your freshman self?" I asked her. She paused, steam rising from her mug. "I would say to her, 'It's going to be different than you expected, but better.'" I nodded in eager agreement at this piece of wisdom. God's plan for our future is often different than we can predict, but better than we could imagine.

We spend our days yearning to live in the present so we don't miss what God has for us here, while also wondering, "Did I say the right thing? Am I living my purpose?" The book *Holy Noticing* explains that our mind is either in direct mode, focusing on a task at hand, or in default mode, where our mind wanders. But day dreaming is not just staring out the window. There are three categories our mind drifts to: distraction, guilt and anxiety, or positive construction, such as goal setting or problem solving.[15] We can go to God in any of these places: noticing His activity in the present, confessing in response to guilt, or dreaming of His future.

Here's what John witnesses about our future: "And I heard a loud voice from the throne saying, 'Behold, the dwelling place of God is with man. He will dwell with them, and they will be his people, and God himself will be with them as their God. He will wipe away every tear from their eyes, and death shall be no more, neither shall there be mourning, nor crying, nor pain anymore, for

---

[15] Stone, *Holy Noticing*, 209.

the former things have passed away'" (Revelation 21:3-4). We can torture ourselves with what the future *might* hold, or we can hold on to what God has already told us.

Fear invades when we dwell on the unknown. Faith blooms when we abide in the known, trusting God to prepare a good future. The struggle is real, but so is God's Word. What He says, He will do, and it will be better than we can imagine. Whatever lies in the future, God has a plan and will protect you in love. Lift your heads, for your redemption is coming. Those tears and fears will be no more.

"He will wipe away every tear from their eyes, and death shall be no more, neither shall there be mourning, nor crying, nor pain anymore, for the former things have passed away" —Revelation 21:3-4

You're about to copy down these words. You know what's coming, all that's left to do is to put pen to paper. May this be practice in trusting God's Word and partnering with Him in the fulfillment of His plans. Now, write the promise above:

_____

_____

_____

1. Name a time when an outcome was different than you expected, but better than you could have imagined.

_____

_____

_____

_____

2. Being anxious about the future is not a sin, but a message. The book *Anxious Kids, Anxious Parents* tells us, "anxiety is a method of seeking two experiences: certainty and comfort. The problem is that it wants these two outcomes immediately and continually."[16] When we aren't immersed in an activity or otherwise engaged, anxiety creeps in and demands the peace of certainty. How does Revelation 21:4 give you both certainty and comfort?

_____

_____

_____

_____

3. What do you worry will happen in the meantime?

_____

_____

_____

_____

[16] Reid Wilson and Lynn Lyons, *Anxious Kids, Anxious Parents: 7 Ways to Stop the Worry Cycle and Raise Courageous and Independent Children* (Deerfield Beach, Florida: Health Communications, Inc. 2013), 88.

4. Revelation 21:4 says, "He will wipe away every tear from their eyes, and death shall be no more, neither shall there be mourning, nor crying, nor pain anymore." Anxiety often tells lies: "You'll *never* get over this," or "You'll *always* be suffering." Who does Scripture say wipes away tears? What anxiety-based lies do you believe? Circle God's promise from this verse that relates to your anxiety and put your trust in the God who knows all.

    _____

    _____

    _____

    _____

5. The rest of verse four says, "For the former things have passed away." The New Living Translation says, "all these things are gone forever." Can you imagine an existence without pain, crying, or death? How does knowing that suffering is temporary give you endurance for a hard season you may be experiencing now?

    _____

    _____

    _____

    _____

6. In her devotional *Jesus Calling*, Sarah Young imagines Jesus saying, "Attentiveness to Me is not only for your quiet time, but for all your time. As you look to Me, I show you what to do now and *next*."[17] Go back to our message for today and review Revelation 21:3. Where does God say He will dwell in the future? What are you doing today to usher in this reality?

_____

_____

_____

_____

7. Revelation 21:5 says, "And he who was seated on the throne said, 'Behold, I am making all things new.' Also he said, 'Write this down, for these words are trustworthy and true.'" Notice the word "making." This suggests that God is in the process of creating the future out of the present. What we trust is what we become (Psalm 135:18). Who is the person you will become if you trust in God for your present moment?

_____

_____

_____

_____

_____

[17] Sarah Young, *Jesus Calling: Enjoying Peace in His Presence* (Nashville: HarperCollins, 2004), 217.

Predictions of the future are everywhere: weather forecasts, financial projections, even medical diagnoses with predicted life expectancies. Once you start seeing them, you'll notice this pattern in your own thoughts as well. Take them with a grain of salt; the salt of the Word, that is. Anchor these predictions with what God's promises say, and put your ultimate trust in His good future. Here are a few examples:

Prediction	Promise
We will start a business and make money.	"If the Lord wills, we will live and do this or that." —James 4:15
The doctor gave me a death sentence.	Jesus is the author of life. —Acts 3:15

Write a brief prayer based on today's reflections:

_____

_____

_____

_____

Spend some time in centering prayer over God's vision of heaven. Hold this image in your heart, and take it with you as a comfort in tough times.

Day 4: Peace Guards Your Heart

The test said, "pregnant," but I knew something was wrong. At the doctor's office, they couldn't see a baby on the ultrasound, but decided to give it two weeks and then follow up. I had a choice. I could research the medical words they gave me for an explanation, but I knew Google couldn't tell me what would happen. When I prayed, the answer I received from God was, "wait." I took a breath. I would not feed my anxiety with *what-ifs*, and felt a strange peace about simply hearing from God. I didn't know what would happen, but I knew God was with me.

As I drove home, I read a bumper sticker that said, "No God, no peace. Know God, know peace." Cheesy *and* true! This week, we covered what we know with absolute certainty for our past, present, and future. The common thread that holds our story together is the presence of God. The resurrection heals our past, God's promises ensure our future, and His Spirit fills the present.

The Bible is very clear: "do not be anxious about anything, but in everything by prayer and supplication with thanksgiving let your requests be made known to God. And the peace of God, which surpasses all understanding, will guard your hearts and your minds in Christ Jesus" (Philippians 4:6-7). Friend, if you don't have peace right now, seek the Lord. This is your invitation. Pray until the peace comes. Pray until your heart softens, your eyes open, and you see God working. And then pray some more. As we would say in Young Life, "prayer *is* the battle." Prayer is our privilege to meet with God: to see life from His perspective, to be secure in His promise, to be held as His child in the middle of the mystery.

I didn't end up having that child, but I felt God mourn with me. I felt His peace and knew that He would make everything okay. I still feel the peace of that experience as I reflect on it, strengthening the center of my faith for all that is to come.

"Do not be anxious about anything, but in everything by prayer and supplication with thanksgiving let your requests be made known to God. And the peace of God, which surpasses all understanding, will guard your hearts and your minds in Christ Jesus." —*Philippians 4:6-7*

Write the verse below, underlining God's instruction to you, and putting brackets around God's promise to you.

_____

_____

_____

_____

1. Share a time when you had peace, despite your world crumbling around you.

_____

_____

_____

_____

2. Paul, the writer of Philippians, had firsthand experience with anxiety. In 2 Corinthians 11:28 he wrote about "the daily pressure on me of anxiety for all the churches." He worried about losing those he loved to the deceit of false gospels (2 Corinthians 11:3). Yet he told the Philippians with complete conviction that the peace of God would guard their hearts and minds in Christ. With the certainty that comes from experience he said, "the Lord is at hand" (Philippians 4:6). Regarding your previous answer, did you sense the closeness of God? How did it impact your peace? Explain:

_____

_____

_____

_____

3. "Do not be anxious about anything, but in everything by prayer and supplication with thanksgiving let your requests be known to God" (Philippians 4:6). The word *prayer* means communicating with God, while *supplication* is a request for a ruler to take action. How does a prayer feel without thanksgiving? How does thanksgiving change our prayer?

_____

_____

_____

_____

4. "The peace of God, which surpasses all understanding..." describes His peace well. We can explain our sense of peace if everything is going well, but peace during hard times is beyond us. This kind of peace comes from a God whose kingdom is not of this world, who dwells in eternal light. A God who is not anxious about anything but who is with His people in everything. How can peace that surpasses our understanding be comforting?

_____

_____

_____

_____

5. Other Bible translations refer to this peace as the kind that "transcends all understanding." The word "transcend" often refers to new age prayer that requires our hard work and dedication to reach higher levels of enlightenment. God's peace is not dependent on us, but is a gift to us. It is His will for us to be at peace in Him. Have you ever been frustrated when you don't receive the feeling of peace from God despite your commitment to seek Him? Did peace eventually arrive? Explain.

_____

_____

_____

_____

6. The peace of God "will guard your hearts and your minds in Christ Jesus" (Philippians 4:7). If our heart is a home, then the walls are its guard. Scripture refers to "walls of Salvation," and "gates of Praise" (Isaiah 60:18). Jesus calls Himself the way, or the gate: "I am the door. If anyone enters by me, he will be saved and will go in and out and find pasture" (John 10:9). How does being bombarded with anxiety cause you to feel vulnerable? How does the peace of Christ make you impervious to any circumstance?

_____

_____

_____

_____

7. How can you let Christ be your guard, your wall of salvation, your gate that decides who comes in and out of your heart and mind?

_____

_____

_____

_____

Author and pastor Max Lucado wisely said, "Expose your worries to an hour of worship...anxiety passes as trust increases."[18] Singing worship is a way to pray with thanksgiving, to "Enter his gates with thanksgiving, and his courts with praise!" (Psalm 100:4). When we worship, we leave our worries behind and head into His heavenly palace, even with our feet on the earth. Spend some time in nothing but worship today, and see how your heart lightens. You can find an *Aligned* worship playlist in the video course at *joyfulhelath.co/aligned*.

Write a brief prayer based on today's reflections:

_____

_____

_____

_____

Spend time in centering prayer, thanking God for the peace we find in Christ.

---

[18] Lucado, *Anxious for Nothing*, 32.

Day 5: Let's Review

Prompt: What do you know? Live upon the promises of God you know to be true for sure.

Promise: *"Do not be anxious about anything, but in everything by prayer and supplication with thanksgiving let your requests be made known to God. And the peace of God, which surpasses all understanding, will guard your hearts and your minds in Christ Jesus." —Philippians 4:6-7*

Recap + Quick Quotes:

This week, we established what we know for sure. By pointing to God's promises, we can rest on our Father's approval, trading our worries of the past for His peace in the present, and look forward to a future better than we can ask or imagine.

- "By praying His promises according to Scripture, God has proven Himself to me beyond a shadow of a doubt time and time again, laying a foundation of solid faith. Knowing I can trust Him gives me comfort to be fully present."
- "How could our anxiety dissipate with the firm knowledge that God has already proven His love toward us?"
- "God's plan for our future is often different than we can predict, but better than we could imagine."
- "Pray until the peace comes. Pray until your heart softens and your eyes open and you can see God working."

Group Discussion Questions:

a. *Main question:* What's one thing that has clicked with you and God this week? How have you experienced His peace in light of this week's study?
b. *Day 1:* What do you know for sure?
c. *Day 2:* When have you had to work for approval? Do you think that impacts your idea of how God views you?
d. *Day 3:* Can you imagine an existence without pain, crying, or death? How does knowing that suffering is temporary give you endurance for a hard season you may be experiencing now?
e. *Day 4:* How can you let Christ be your guard, your wall of salvation, your gate that decides who comes in and out of your heart and mind?
f. *Bonus question:* What doubts most often plague your mind about belief in God and what He says to be true?

Prayer:

Lord,
We thank you for your patience with us as we wrestle with what we know for sure. In a world that does not uphold absolute truth, we can trust that even when we falter, you will continue to be faithful. Like Thomas, we might ask to see your hands and feet, to see physical signs of Your existence. May you strengthen our hearts to believe, even when we do not see. As we close our eyes and shut down our visual dependence, may we know You with our spirit. Speak to us in the silence. We take the next few minutes to listen. [Let two minutes pass.] Amen.

Group Prayer Requests

_____

_____

_____

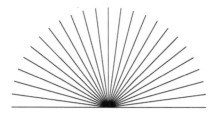

Session 6: Learn to Let the Rest Go

O God and Heavenly Father, Grant to us the serenity of mind to accept that which cannot be changed; the courage to change that which can be changed, and wisdom to know the one from the other, through Jesus Christ our Lord, Amen. —*Reinhold Niebuh, Serenity Prayer*

Day 1: Let Go of What You Don't Have

When I was in high school, a cheer mom gave me an angel with the inscription: "Blessed are the Meek." I was appreciative, but couldn't help feeling like meek was weak. I didn't want to be weak! I was already sensitive, but meekness felt shy and mousy. I was disappointed because I thought I needed what the world values: grit and gumption. But the world couldn't offer peace. Only God offers peace, and only the meek can receive it. The Serenity Prayer invites us to accept that which we cannot change, and we can only be content in God's ways when we receive His gifts with meekness.

In a culture that affirms that everyone "deserves to be happy," we develop greedy attitudes. Or at least, I certainly do! Instead of accepting the blessings God gave us, we may blame our unhappiness on what we don't have. God promises that "the meek shall inherit the land and delight themselves in abundant peace" (Psalm 37:11). The meek are set apart. The meek let go of what they don't have and accept what God has given them. God makes everything beautiful in its time, and the meek have eyes to see it.

Do we have the strength to be grateful for what we have right this moment? Instead of berating our bodies for aging, may we delight in nourishing the only body we will inhabit on earth. Instead of rushing to the next season, may we see cherish opportunities in this unique point of time. Instead of coveting a neighbor's success, job promotion, nice house, or well-behaved kids, may we enjoy, honor, and steward our own inheritance of love given to us by God.

Instead of feeling entitled, may we be joyful in acceptance. We can chase the world's images of happiness, but as French poet Guillaume Apollinaire said, "Now and then it's good to pause in our pursuit of happiness and just be happy." This is what it feels like to let go of expectations and accept what God has for us now. Let's stop squinting for signs while chasing someone else's happy, become meek, and simply receive the gift of God's message. Blessed are the meek.

"But the meek shall inherit the land and delight themselves in abundant peace." —Psalm 37:11

As you sit down to write, give thanks for the writing surface God has given you, the pen, the paper, hands to write with, the space you are inhabiting. This is yours to enjoy. Go ahead and write the above promise with gratitude:

_____

_____

_____

1. What does our culture feel entitled to? What do we feel like we each deserve? Can you give examples of how this is communicated through marketing, social media, or other avenues?

_____

_____

_____

2. What is something you feel you deserve but have not received? Is it making you unhappy?

_____

_____

_____

_____

3. Psalm 37:10 says the reign of the wicked is temporary—one day they are here, and the next they are not. But the meek who look to the Lord have what those who are self-focused can never buy: peace that surpasses understanding. Is there someone you envy? Consider the long view. How is comparing yourself to this person stealing the joy God offers you now?

_____

_____

_____

_____

4. The word "meek" in Psalm 37:11 contrasts the proud and haughty. The proud may possess acres but only want more, and therefore not truly enjoy what he has. The meek person is the humble, gentle, contented servant and friend of God who waits for and delights in Him alone. The meek servant is happy in God, and everything else is simply a gift. This is the

only kind of person who can inherit the land and fully enjoy what God gives. Ecclesiastes 4:6 says, "Better is a handful of quietness than two hands full of toil and striving after wind." In what area of your life do you always want more, but it is never enough? How could an attitude of meekness change that?

_____

_____

_____

5. The meek accept that everything comes from the Lord: "Look at what God has made. You cannot change a thing, even if you think it is wrong. When life is good, enjoy it. But when life is hard, remember that God gives us good times and hard times" (Ecclesiastes 7:13 ERV). Even in hard times, God gives us the promise that these days are temporary and numbered, while eternal peace lasts forever.

    This also is from the Lord, and far outweighs any affliction we might face, infusing every moment with the light of His glory. Is there something out of your hands that you have not considered part of God's plans for good? Bring it to the Lord. There is power in lament because it's an invitation to bring our discontent to God, bringing us closer to Him and to the peace that comes with trusting Him with all things.

_____

_____

_____

6. The meek shall "delight themselves in abundant peace" which cannot be bought, measured, or hoarded. It is more than we can ask for, and better than we can imagine! Those who are meek of heart are aligned with God's peace, peace of mind, and peace with others. The meek do not strive to seize that which is not theirs, but fully accept that all things are from God. Where or when have you experienced this kind of peace? Describe your situation and the sense of peace.

_____

_____

_____

_____

7. This Psalm is the precursor to Jesus' promise in the Beatitudes: "Blessed are the meek, for they shall inherit the earth" (Matthew 5:5). Rather than seize the day, we receive the Lord. All things were given into Jesus' hands (John 3:35), and all things are ours in Christ (1 Corinthians 3:21-23). We can let go of the world's ambition and instead rest in the quiet identity as royal children of the most high, serving with love in humility because He gives the earth to those who are meek, not to those who work. What fears does the rest of the world have about our responsibility to the earth? What does God say instead?

_____

_____

_____

When we consider the present moment as something we receive as an undeserved gift of grace, we can laugh with the joy of the Lord, who gives generously beyond our wildest expectations. We will be like the Israelites, oppressed and finally delivered: "Then our mouth was filled with laughter, and our tongue with shouts of joy; then they said among the nations, 'The Lord has done great things for them'" (Psalm 126:2). We will be like Sarah, who laughed when God made her an unbelievable promise. Laughter is joy taking us by surprise.

Take time to lighten up today and enjoy the amazing gifts God has given you, even if it takes a fake laugh to turn into a real laugh. You just might find your shoulders releasing tension, your breath deepening, and the peace returning. The meek will inherit the earth.

Write a brief prayer based on today's reflections:

_____

_____

_____

_____

Spend a moment in centering prayer. As expectations crop up like clouds, seek the sun and God's ever-steady presence.

Day 2: Let Go of What Is Not Yours to Own

"I want to write books, but I *can't*," I said with tears in my eyes. "Why not?" my husband said, leaning over the metal table at our outdoor lunch date. "Because I have to keep up with the blog. I asked friends to write for it, and now I can't leave them hanging. People are *counting on me*." As the words came out, I realized I wasn't sure which blog followers would actually miss my online presence. "Just quit," he said simply. "Just *quit*?" The thought of being a *quitter* made my stomach feel queasy, but the idea of letting the blog go felt like a weight lifted off my shoulders. And that's when it hit me: I was no longer owning this responsibility, it was owning me. If we want to align with God's peace, we need to let go of what is owning us, and allow God to make us His own.

Letting go is scary, particularly when peace of mind is wrapped up in what we think we need. But what if you already have what you need for eternity, and know it can't be taken away from you? I needed to be the responsible person—or at least, that's who I thought I needed to be. What I needed most was to realize that even when I let go, God holds on. God gave me the message and motivation to write another book, but my inability to release responsibility got in the way.

While we white-knuckle our roles and responsibilities, God longs to set us apart for His purposes: "Now may the God of peace himself sanctify you completely, and may your whole spirit and soul and body be kept blameless at the coming of our Lord Jesus Christ" (1 Thessalonians 5:23). God will make us complete. We do not become whole by adding more but by giving our life away to the Lord.

When I quit the blog, an error caused years of content to be deleted. It was a reckoning for me. But the good news? The absence of my work did not take away who I was, but reminded me of what actually matters. When God is all you have, you have all you need. When we let go, we have nothing to lose! Try it out: let go of what weighs you down and you'll find God is the one holding you up. You'll not only feel lighter, but also be aligned with who God is making you to be.

"Now may the God of peace himself sanctify you completely, and may your whole spirit and soul and body be kept blameless at the coming of our Lord Jesus Christ." —1 Thessalonians 5:23

Write down this prayer as if you were Paul writing to those God meant it for. Put yourself in his shoes, and with compassion and a tender heart, write as if this is truly God's will for you, too.

_____

_____

_____

1. What are you holding that feels like it owns you, but you can't seem to release?

_____

_____

_____

2. Is your inability to let go preventing you from doing something else? In her book *The Next Right Thing*, Emily Freeman says, "desire is only toxic when we demand our desires be satisfied on our terms and in our timing. Knowing what we want and getting what we want are not necessarily the same thing...Honor your design and image-bearing identity enough to be honest about what you want most."[19] Is there a greater desire God is growing in you?

_____

_____

_____

_____

3. Our verse today introduces "the God of peace himself." God makes things whole, heals our ailments, and connects essential parts. He is essential for your identity now and who you will become in the future, so be at peace knowing He is the one who discerns what is best for you. What does it mean for God to be described as the "God of peace himself"?

_____

_____

_____

_____

---

[19] Emily Freeman, *The Next Right Thing: A Simple, Soulful Practice for Making Life Decisions* (Grand Rapids, Michigan: Revell, 2019), 88-89.

4. For God to "sanctify you completely," he sets you apart as dedicated to God and His purpose, making you whole and holy. If you were able to let go of your answer from question one, how could you be more dedicated to God and His purposes?

_____

_____

_____

_____

5. Elsewhere, Paul refers to only "body and spirit," while here, he prays for the "whole spirit and soul and body be kept blameless." The spirit here refers to the part of us which comprehends God intuitively, while the soul includes our affections, ambitions, and intelligence. We need God to unite, integrate, and align all parts of us to finish the good work of redemption He started through Christ. Is there anything you're refusing to hand over to the Lord: spirit, soul, or body? What's holding you back?

_____

_____

_____

_____

_____

6. Of spirit, soul, or body, which have you been putting more emphasis on at the expense of the others?

_____

_____

_____

_____

7. Our formation will be completed "at the coming of our Lord Jesus Christ," the final test of our character in Christ. This reminder is not to scare us, but to comfort us in the reminder that it is God who works in us. That work is completed when He transforms us from one degree of glory to another. How can releasing the circumstance you mentioned in question one prepare you for the Lord's coming?

_____

_____

_____

_____

Freedom lies in forgetting ourselves and following Christ to gain what we cannot lose. Like a sculpture hidden within a chunk of rock, our choices sculpt our shape. What could you allow the Lord to chip off that would leave you feeling at peace? Just as a sculptor chisels off small pieces of a time, be patient and take away one small thing today.

Write a prayer based on today's reflections:

_____

_____

_____

_____

Spend some time in centering prayer, focusing on your exhale. As your body filters through oxygen and takes what you need for life, your lungs also let go of the carbon dioxide you don't need. Be reminded with every exhale that this process of letting go is a natural part of life.

Day 3: Let Go of Clutter for Kingdom Clarity

Overcrowded gardens don't grow well. My first few forays into gardening started out big: I got about seven tomato plants, zucchinis, cucumbers, carrots, herbs of all kinds, even watermelon! My logic was: "Let's just try 'em all and see what grows!" The problem was, our family didn't even eat the types of food I planted. But my sister had sent me pictures of her abundant zucchini and squash harvest and I thought that's what every garden needed: a lot of options. That's what gets me into trouble—wanting too many things and feeling anxious about them all. I needed to let go of unrealistic expectations, grow what I could handle, and plant what we liked. I was in charge of what to grow! This applies to the garden of our mind as well. God is the gardener, and knows how to sow the best plants. May His kingdom grow in us, starting with a clear plot of grace, the vine of Christ, and the wisdom and discernment of the Spirit.

The church of the Romans had a cluttered garden of ideas too, and instead of growing together in Christ, people were struggling for dominance. Mixed segments of Jewish and Gentile people argued over rules and expectations. Should Christians eat meat? Should they fast on a certain day? What about hand washing? Paul, in the book of Romans, pulls the weeds and plants a vision of becoming aligned on matters of the kingdom: "For the kingdom of God is not a matter of eating and drinking but of righteousness and peace and joy in the Holy Spirit" (Romans 14:17). What doesn't matter in the kingdom shouldn't matter to us either. We can let go of heavy expectations, worn-out rules, and social norms that don't align with the gospel. Once we know what kingdom growth is about, we can uproot the rest.

When I consulted my neighbor about my garden, she said, "If you plant too much, leave the plants that are growing well and pull the extras." Pull baby carrots? They're just babies! But when I took a step back to assess, she was right. The garden was suffocating. I pulled stunted plants and created space. I went inside and evaluated my life priorities too, feeling the freedom to cancel current commitments and leave what yielded peace and joy. These would grow into kingdom fruit that lasted—I could feel it.

"For the kingdom of God is not a matter of eating and drinking but of righteousness and peace and joy in the Holy Spirit." —Romans 14:17

Write down today's promise, then strike through "eating and drinking." Underline the first letters of "righteousness, peace, and joy" to help you memorize what the kingdom is about (RPJ). Then circle "in the Holy Spirit" to emphasize our source:

_____

_____

1. What area of your life feels cluttered?

_____

_____

_____

_____

2. "Your most crucial environment is neither external nor internal: it is eternal, for you are in Christ."[20] The environment of our mind and heart is where we live and what we filter our lives through. What grows around you where you live? Describe the plants, the animals, and the environment that affects each of them. If you could compare the garden of your mind to a specific biome (rainforest, tundra, desert, etc.), which would you choose for your current state, and why?

_____

_____

_____

_____

3. The privilege of Christian freedom is the right to reject or receive ideas into our conscience on the basis of love. Jesus should be the gate of entry and exit for the garden of our minds and hearts. In Romans 14, Paul discouraged believers to pass judgment on each other, "so then each of us will give an account of himself to God" (Romans 14:12). Nobody

_____

[20] Denise Hughes and Cheri Gregory, *Sensitive and Strong: A Guide for Highly Sensitive Persons and Those Who Love Them* (Eugene: Harvest House Publishers), 90.

else knows what's really going on inside the other. Each one of us lives "coram deo," before the presence of God. We live under His authority and for His glory alone. What other voices or thoughts are crowding the space of your heart? Are you listening to them or to the Lord? How can you tell the difference?

_____

_____

_____

_____

4. The first part of Romans 14:17 says, "For the kingdom of God is not a matter of eating and drinking." We will indeed feast in the kingdom together, but it will be in the spirit of communion so we may have peace with one another. We are not better or worse than another for our eating and drinking choices. Even when we don't agree on cultural rules, our peace is in Christ, who has broken down the walls: "For he himself is our peace, who has made us both one and has broken down in his flesh the dividing wall of hostility" (Ephesians 2:14). What cultural rule around food, health, or something else do you disagree with? How can Jesus be your neutral ground?

_____

_____

_____

_____

5. The kingdom of God is a matter of "righteousness and peace and joy in the Holy Spirit" (Romans 14:17b). This joy arises from being made right through the forgiveness of sins, and resting in the knowledge that grace means we no longer have to strive in our own works. How can you let go of extraneous rules and allow the kingdom to grow in your mind and heart?

_____

_____

6. What is taking up space that doesn't belong in the kingdom of love? Think about cultural expectations and social norms, generational traditions and media trends. Take them off the throne and put them onto the altar. We cannot serve two gods at once, and when we allow God to sit on the throne and be the chief gardener, he brings the peace of rightly ordered affections.

As Richard Foster says in his book, _The Celebration of Discipline_, "Simplicity is freedom. Duplicity is bondage. Simplicity brings joy and balance. Duplicity brings anxiety and fear. The preacher of Ecclesiastes observes that 'God made man simple; man's complex problems are of his own devising' (Ecclesiastes 7:30, JB)."[21] What problems are you entertaining that have no place with you and God?

_____

_____

_____

---

[21] Richard J. Foster, _Celebration of Discipline: The Path to Spiritual Growth_ (New York: HarperCollins, 1978), 80.

_____

_____

7. Integrity is doing what we believe, aligning ourselves with the truth. The last part of this chapter of Romans says, "For whatever does not proceed from faith is sin" (Romans 14:23). Doing anything outside of faith is like an invasive species that burdens the whole ecosystem. Compare decisions you've made based on outside pressure versus internal conviction. Which one brings peace, and why?

_____

_____

_____

What area of your life feels cluttered by anxiety? The best way to organize a space is to take everything out, then consciously and prayerfully choose what you'd like to add that aligns with the kingdom values of righteousness, peace, and joy. Write down your plans below:

I will spend _____ minutes clearing out

_____

_____

_____

on this date _____.

Spend a moment in centering prayer, focusing on the words "righteousness, peace, and joy," and letting go of every other thought.

Day 4: Let Go of Uncertainty and Ask for Wisdom

I could hear footsteps as they all clambered in the kitchen for dinner. I tried to read their faces as they approached the table and braced myself for the usual "Ugh, gross! I can't eat that!" reaction from the kids. I had made one homemade meal that everyone loved, a hamburger helper, but I couldn't remember which recipe it was. None I scrolled through looked familiar. I cooked the meal the best I could, but I really didn't know if it was going to be edible or not. While I was wringing my hands in worry, I could have been tasting the meal as I went along. Many times, the solution to worry is to ask what's right by taking wise action.

I've heard that "knowledge is knowing that a tomato is a fruit. Wisdom is knowing not to put it in a fruit salad." Although the source of this maxim is debatable, the truth is not. We need discernment about what to keep and what to let go (and where to put it). Our focus for this week is centered around the Serenity Prayer: gracefully accepting what is not ours to change, the courage to change what we need to own, and wisdom to know the difference. Biblical wisdom is personified as a woman: "Long life is in her right hand; in her left hand are riches and honor. Her ways are ways of pleasantness, and all her paths are peace. She is a tree of life to those who lay hold of her; those who hold her fast are called blessed" (Proverbs 3:16-18). The best way to let go of anxiety is to hold fast to peace with both hands, letting all else go.

Our role is not to know all things, but in uncertainty the Lord invites us to seek, to ask, to knock. Lady wisdom is waiting!

Sometimes, the answer we need is only a question away. I could have tasted that meal as I went. But what I really wanted out of that meal was to nourish my kids, to connect around the table, to be a good mom. Instead of wondering, I went ahead and asked my child: "What can I do to be a better mom today?" Her answer? "Maybe a hug." So simple. So sweet. Anxiety complicates things. May we have the serenity to know what is good, and the boldness to ask for what we seek and take action. Our Heavenly Father holds out His hands to us all day. When we reach out in prayer, our hands will meet, our hearts will align with the light of truth.

"Long life is in her right hand; in her left hand are riches and honor. Her ways are ways of pleasantness, and all her paths are peace. She is a tree of life to those who lay hold of her; those who hold her fast are called blessed." —Proverbs 3:16-18

Write today's promise, then hold out your hands. Instead of wondering what you should pick up with them today, imagine placing them in the hands of wisdom, and going from there.

---

1. Have you ever held on to something for too long, not sure where you should put it so it just accumulated dust?

_____

_____

2. Sometimes what we hold is not an object, but a decision, anxiety, or fear. Instead of carrying it with you, take the opportunity to ask God what to do. Ask for wisdom. James 1:5 says, "If any of you lacks wisdom, let him ask God, who gives generously to all without reproach, and it will be given him." Underline the words that stick out to you in this verse, and write down a time when you need wisdom:

_____

_____

_____

_____

_____

3. Proverbs 3:16 says, "Long life is in her right hand; in her left hand are riches and honor." In the Bible, the right side is typically associated with obedience. Good health for a long life is the blessing of wholeness and enjoyment, which represents the fulfillment of the law. Today, this is fulfilled in Christ. The left hand represents the consequences of going our own way, but here, wisdom offers blessings of going with God. Wealth and reputation refer to the riches of Christ and the honor given to us by Him in faith. Using your answer from question two, in which category would you place your

need for wisdom, the right hand or the left? Health and enjoyment, provision and approval, or both?

_____

_____

_____

_____

4. Let's move to Proverbs 3:17: "Her ways are ways of pleasantness, and all her paths are peace." Ellicott's Commentary says, "Peace is the highest reward of the New Testament for the life of thankful dependence upon God."[22] Isn't that the truth? When we walk in the wisdom of the Lord, we are assured in all our ways. According to the commentary, the "way" is *the highway,* and the "path" is the *byway.* Both are paved with peace. Most of our goals in life have happiness as the destination, but with wisdom, peace and joyfulness accompanies us as we travel the path. We don't have to wait until heaven to experience the fruit of confidence in Christ. Referencing your answer from question two again, would you say you need peace for the long-term or purpose for the short-term? Or do you need both?

_____

_____

_____

[22] "Proverbs 3:17 Commentaries," Bible Hub, accessed March 20, 2023, https://biblehub.com/commentaries/proverbs/3-17.htm

5. The *Berean Study Bible* translates Proverbs 3:18a this way: "She is a tree of life to those who embrace her." Compare the tree of life to the tree of the knowledge of good and evil from Genesis 3. What was the outcome of consuming the fruit of the latter? Consider that God allows us to eat from the tree of life, the tree of wisdom, who is Christ. One gives life, one takes it away. How can you align yourself with what is life-giving for your situation?

_____

_____

_____

_____

6. "Those who hold her fast are called blessed," says the rest of Proverbs 3:18. The word "blessed" means "happy." The tree of the knowledge of good and evil allows us to define good and evil for ourselves. Does making decisions based on our own judgment typically make us happy or lead to peace? How about when we honor the Lord, the beginning of all wisdom?

_____

_____

_____

_____

7. We may try to hold on to a decision or a responsibility because we want to control the outcome, which is usually futile. We can choose what to believe and how to behave in response. In a circle below, write down what you can do in your situation based on today's exercises, and write down what you can let go of outside of the circle.

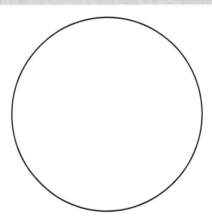

Jesus wants us to cast all of our anxieties on Him because He cares for us (1 Peter 5:7). Hold your hands like you are holding a worry. Now lift your hands up into the air like you're tossing it up to the Lord. Do this physically every time you are stressed or unsure. And if you come from a conservative background like me, this is good practice to surrender in worship! When our bodies act in symphony with our mind and heart, we feel integrated, aligned, unified, and peaceful. We will find rest and peace in God when we let go of what is not ours to carry. Rest in your role as His child, and in His role as our wise Father.

Write a brief prayer based on today's reflections:

_____

_____

Spend time in centering prayer on the floor. Be reminded that we don't carry the weight of the world on our shoulders, but the earth holds us up by gravity. Let God hold you here in this moment.

Day 5: Let's Review

Prompt: What can you let go of? What is not yours to own, but to entrust to God?

Promise: *"But the meek shall inherit the land and delight themselves in abundant peace." —Psalm 37:11*

Recap + Quick Quotes:

This week, we hold fast to God's Word, that which lasts in love, and discover the freedom to let go of the rest.

- "The Serenity Prayer invites us to accept that which we cannot change. We can only be content in God's ways when we receive His gifts with the quiet satisfaction of meekness."
- "If we want to be aligned with God's peace, we need to let go of what is owning us, and allow God to make us His own."
- "We can let go of heavy expectations, worn-out rules, and social norms that don't align with the gospel. Once we know what kingdom growth is about, we can leave the rest."
- "Anxiety is not ours to carry. Wisdom is knowing God has the answers, and exercising the boldness to approach the throne of grace with confidence."

Group Discussion Questions:

    a. *Main question:* What's one thing that has clicked with you and God this week? How have you experienced His peace?

    b. *Day 1:* What does our culture feel entitled to? Can you give examples of how this is communicated through marketing, social media, and other outlets?

    c. *Day 2:* Is there a desire God is growing in you, but you feel you can't pursue because of an obstacle? What is in the way?

    d. *Day 3:* We live under God's authority and for His glory alone. What other voices or thoughts crowd the space of your heart? Are you listening to them or to the Lord? How can you tell the difference?

    e. *Day 4:* Share about what's within your control, and what you need to let go.

    f. *Bonus question:* What has been hard for you to let go of this week? Control? Perfectionism? Responsibility that is not yours to own?

Prayer:

Lord,

Thank you for saving us. In our salvation, we have nothing to lose. You say that when we lose our lives for Your sake, we will save them. You say it is better to take out our eye if it causes us to sin than for our whole selves to be destroyed. Give us a single-minded passion for Your word, a singular vision for Your kingdom love, and the peace to let the rest go. You are all we need. We submit to you the next two minutes in silent prayer. Center us on Your light, and let the rest fade away. We come to You now. [Let two minutes pass.] Amen.

Group Prayer Requests

_____

_____

_____

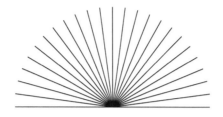

Session 7: Take the Next Step

Stayed on Omnipotence, safe 'neath His wing,
Leave all results, do the next thing.
Minnie E. Paull in Ye Nexte Thynge

Day 1: When in Doubt, Go in Peace

My friend Sabrena had a difficult birth experience followed by depression, the need for physical therapy, and PTSD counseling. After much prayer, the desire to have another baby blossomed alongside her growing toddler. It also opened the door to fear and anxiety. *Could she endure labor and delivery again?* One provider told her it would be worse the second time around and described the physical challenges, including possible permanent damage if she decided to have another child. Still, she kept her heart open, let the feelings wash over, and explored options. She sought the counsel of another provider, friends surrounded her in prayer, and she said...yes! Unfortunately, it sometimes takes walking with God through the valley to learn how to fear no evil. We do not let fear and anxiety rule over us, but let God's Word reign and go forth.

Our enemy often uses anxiety as a diversion to distract us from reality. He is called "the prince of the power of the air," (Ephesians 2:2) and can lead us astray with deception, but cannot create life. Jesus, on the other hand, is the Prince of Peace, and creates everything visible out of which is invisible. In Genesis, He makes all that we can see out of His wisdom. In Ezekiel, He puts flesh on dry bones and makes an army of the Lord. In the gospels, He creates peace by His body and blood. And now, He equips us with the armor of God and puts the gospel of peace as shoes for our feet. His Word proclaims: "How beautiful upon the mountains are the feet of him who brings good news, who publishes peace, who brings good news of happiness, who publishes salvation, who says to Zion, 'Your God reigns'" (Isaiah 52:7). What He says, goes.

Eight months after Sabrena said "yes," she was pregnant. "I felt at peace because I knew the Savior was going before me. My first experience taught me so much about myself, the Lord, and about His nearness to those who are in suffering. I wouldn't want to go through that again, but I wouldn't trade it. I knew that God would be there with me." She calls this experience beautiful, and now gets to shout to us: "Your God reigns!" Don't let anxiety keep you. Let it go, and let's go.

"How beautiful upon the mountains are the feet of him who brings good news, who publishes peace, who brings good news of happiness, who publishes salvation, who says to Zion, 'Your God reigns!'" — Isaiah 52:7

Take a look at your feet (yes, your feet!) and say, as silly as it might seem, "The Lord calls you beautiful. Let's go bring the good news." Now write the promise from above down until you believe it:

_____

_____

_____

1. What anxious thoughts hold you back from something potentially life-changing? What is that anxiety saying?

_____

_____

_____

2. What does God's Word say in response? The peace you gain is worth anything you could lose. What are you afraid of losing? Explain a time when you were nervous or in the middle of the unknown, but walked in faith and experienced the peace of God.

_____

_____

_____

3. The context for Isaiah 52:7 is a proclamation of freedom for the Jews from the captivity of Babylon, and for us, it translates into freedom from sin. Babylon is the ancient image of an evil, worldly system counterfeit to God's legitimate kingdom. While we no longer live in captivity to a literal Babylon, we remain slaves to sin (John 8:34). A nineteenth-century English scholar, Bishop B. F. Westcott said, "There are three tenses of salvation: you have been set free from the penalty of sin, you are being set free from the power of sin and you will be set free from the presence of sin."[23] What sin still has power over you? You may feel heaviness in your spirit but not be able to pinpoint it. Ask the Lord to search your heart, to test you and know your anxious thoughts, and lead you to the way everlasting (Psalm 139:23). Write where you still feel captive:

_____

_____

_____

---

[23] Bishop B.F. Westcott, as quoted in https://www.bible.com/reading-plans/17704-bible-in-one-year-2020-with-nicky-gumbel/day/257

4. This verse is an echo of Isaiah 40:9, where Zion was the proclaimer of good news. Now good news is being brought to Zion herself, telling her that God truly reigns. Christians are preachers of the good news, but we too need the good news. Where do you have a hard time believing that God reigns? Consider how Jesus' ministry proves God's kingdom has come to earth.

_____

_____

_____

_____

5. How beautiful are the feet upon the mountains! Messengers in those days would run for miles, kicking up dust and arriving dirty. This is what God calls beautiful: someone who is covered in muck, yet runs with the zeal of good news. Jesus says that we are clean. We need only to wash our feet (John 13:10). Jesus washes our feet, and then we wash each other's. How can the message of peace God gives allow you to bring the beauty of the gospel to others in their messy spaces? Consider how this picture allows you to run your mission with joy, with perfect peace guarding your heart and mind.

_____

_____

_____

_____

6. To publish peace and salvation means to write what is already true. Take the pressure off yourself. It is not yours to create peace, but to proclaim it! We get to say to Zion, "Your God reigns!" Matthew Henry's commentary says, "The gospel proclaims liberty to those bound with fears. Let those weary and heavy laden under the burden of sin, find relief in Christ, shake themselves from the dust of their doubts and fears, and loose themselves from those bands."[24] How does the good news allow you to shake off the dust of fear and doubt? What do you need to do to walk in faith today?

_____

_____

_____

_____

What gets your heart racing, what makes you come alive? For me, it's running. I warm up, run as fast as I can until I feel like I'm flying, run out of steam, recover, and do it all over again. I have a playlist full of inspirational songs, and I truly feel the joy of the Lord when I run, *Chariots of Fire* style. Running is how I experience God's freedom, and after I get home, I'm ready to bring the good news! I don't always love social media, but after a run I want to shout from the rooftops how good God is. I care less about myself and more about sharing what I've found. I want to tell everyone they don't have to feel alone, that He is here with us, reigning, running to bring you the good news: He has won the

---

[24] "Isaiah 52:7 Commentaries." Bible Hub. Accessed March 20, 2023. https://biblehub.com/commentaries/isaiah/52-7.htm

war! You need to know this. Write down the movement or activity that makes you feel the joy of the Lord. Use it to break out of anxiety, and metaphorically (or literally) run with that momentum. Let your feet carry the good news as far as God will take you, down the streets of your city, past the airwaves of the internet, and beyond, until the whole earth is filled with the glory of the Lord! This is the great commission, and anxiety can't stop this army. We won't stop until everyone has been set free, amen?

Instead of writing a prayer here, go and do the activity that makes you feel free, and then share how God is setting you free. Be a prayer in action!

When you have a quiet moment, spend a few breaths in centering prayer, rejoicing in the truth that "our God reigns!" and the promise that His reign is yet to come.

Day 2: Walk Humbly

They say don't fly too close to the sun. But I wasn't flying close to the sun, I was racing it. Getting up at five o'clock in the morning was the only way I could be on time to teach my 5:30 a.m. fitness class. Writing from 11:30 p.m. until 1:30 a.m. was my only uninterrupted time to write my book. Not surprisingly, there were consequences. My body told me I needed a solid nine hours of sleep to feel capable of meeting my daily demands, but my anxiety said that was preposterous. I needed to hustle if I wanted to be successful. Looking back on it, the only thing I was succeeded in was meeting my own deadlines. But I was dying inside. I felt resentful. When we push the limits for our own sake, we not only crowd out peace, but become misaligned with the central place of growth with the Lord.

What about ambition? What about believing God can do bigger things than we are capable of? Here's what the Bible says about the path to inner peace, and it doesn't look anything like climbing a ladder: "O Lord, my heart is not lifted up; my eyes are not raised too high; I do not occupy myself with things too great and too marvelous for me. But I have calmed and quieted my soul, like a weaned child with its mother; like a weaned child is my soul within me. O Israel, hope in the Lord from this time forth and forevermore" (Psalm 131:1-3). I was living like I was above the laws of nature, and my inner tantrums revealed my pride and lack of trust in God's creation and continued care.

We must decrease, he must increase. And sometimes, that means stripping away all that causes us to sin to return to the peace we have sought all along. I told my fitness director I needed to step back from teaching the early morning class so I could get more sleep. Outside of having babies, I haven't been off the fitness schedule for more than twelve years. Over the summer, I allowed myself to sleep in. It felt good. I didn't have to work so hard to feel peaceful when I consistently lived within my physical limits. I'm choosing to walk humbly with my God, and I trust He will give me what I need. Walking in humility is trusting God with our boundaries, experiencing the joy of freedom within them, and having peace that comes with knowing Christ.

"But I have calmed and quieted my soul, like a weaned child with its mother; like a weaned child is my soul within me." —Psalm 131:2

Take a deep breath, and exhale until you have no more breath. This helps regulate rogue emotions. Write the promise below:

_____

_____

_____

_____

1. What ambition is causing you to act in ways that are not who you want to be in the Lord?

_____

_____

_____

2. Peace is too great a cost when it comes to pushing ourselves outside of the Lord's guidance. What can you do to take care of that need in a loving way?

_____

_____

3. The whole of Psalm 131 consists of three verses, as quoted in today's devotional. It's an entire chapter devoted to calm, quiet trust. When our needs are met consistently, we develop trust. The three needs every human being is born with is to feel seen, soothed, and safe.[25] We can learn to live without one of these three for a time, but we must return to our window of tolerance (WOT) to stay healthy. I learned about the window of tolerance in the book *Try Softer*. Author Aundi Kolber explains that "when we are in our window, the brain stays integrated with the prefrontal cortex, which allows us to pay compassionate attention to ourselves to try softer."[26] Some activities release joy and energy, while others drain us. What symptoms signify that you are pushing past the threshold of your WOT? What activities or situations encourage you and expand your tolerance, and which ones cause you to shrink back?

_____

_____

_____

[25] Tina Payne Bryson, PhD, "When Children Feel Safe, Seen, and Soothed (Most of the Time), They Develop Security," January 9, 2020, www.tinabryson.com/news/when-children-feel-safe-seen-amp-soothed-most-of-the-time-they-develop-security.
[26] Aundi Kolber, *Try Softer: A Fresh Approach to Move Us out of Anxiety, Stress, and Survival Mode--and into a Life of Connection and Joy* (Carol Stream, Illinois: Tyndale, 2020), page 72

_____

_____

4. We want great and glorious things. This explains our hunger for ambition that only the pursuit of God can fill. But we must be moldable, ready to follow Him into any given task, great or small. The title of Psalm 131, "I Have Calmed and Quieted My Soul," is like an echo to 2 Samuel 6:21[27], when David danced before the Lord with all His might in lowly priestly garments instead of King's apparel. His wife disdained him for this. But David trusted God, and in time, became king. God's ways of exaltation always come through humility: "Whoever exalts himself will be humbled, and whoever humbles himself will be exalted" (Matthew 23:12). Nobody is excluded from this spiritual law. Even Jesus submitted himself to this way of life. What situation has humbled you, and how has God lifted you up?

_____

_____

_____

_____

5. When we calm and quiet our soul, like a weaned child with its mother, we are able to trust that God is near and can give us what we need. My hope is that you will see God deliver on His promises, every time. Do you feel your soul

---

[27] "Psalm 131 OT Commentary." Bible Hub. Accessed March 20, 2023. https://biblehub.com/commentaries/kad/psalms/131.htm

calm within you? If not, what are you crying out for that God can satisfy?

_____

_____

_____

6. "I do not occupy myself with things too great or marvelous to me" (Psalm 131:1) refers to matters outside of our hands. Concerning ourselves with things not meant for us causes striving within and strife without. David, the author of Psalm 131, did not seize the priestly role like his predecessor Saul, but was faithful to the Lord's plans. This phrase is also related to David's son, Solomon, who prayed for wisdom and understanding to lead the people. What "great and marvelous" things do you need to let go of and allow God to handle? Where do you need wisdom when you feel you are in over your head?

_____

_____

7. The conclusion of Psalm 131 encourages Israel to hope in the Lord, now and forevermore. Waiting quietly for God doesn't mean your feet are still, but that your heart is calm. Is there anything else you are hoping for outside of the Lord?

_____

_____

Your exercise in humility is to submit yourself to the low spaces of your life, learning faithfulness in the small things. Here's the best way to do that: chores. Yes! Chores are one way to partner with God, practicing humility with a grateful heart behind the scenes. This exercise comes from the book *Raising Worry-Free Girls* by Sissy Goff:

"When you give [your daughter] responsibilities, you're reminding her that she's capable of fulfilling those responsibilities. She is capable. Chores are actually empowering for kids! Help her find her way to purpose too. When she gives of herself, she'll experience not only a sense of fulfillment but also a sense of confidence. Confidence and anxiety are antithetical to each other."[28] Chores are not just activities to dread, but could be the training ground God uses to grow each of His daughters and sons in humility. As Mother Teresa says, "Not all of us can do great things. But we can do small things with great love."

Spend a moment in centering prayer, strengthening your calm soul.

[28] Sissy Goff and Carlos Whittaker, *Raising Worry-Free Girls: Helping Your Daughter Feel Braver, Stronger, and Smarter in an Anxious World* (Bloomington, Illinois: Bethany House Publishers, 2019), 129.

Day 3: Blessed are the Peacemakers

There's little else that causes more stress and anxiety than misaligned relationships. For Emily, it was her family. Whenever it was time to go to her in-laws' house, her anxiety would spike. She would walk on eggshells when she was there and worry about what would happen when she returned. The tension built with no release in sight. She and her husband decided the next visit would include a direct conversation. *How would her in-laws react? Where would they go from here?* Their pastor stepped in for support and attended the meeting. She could breathe a little easier. There was no immediate resolution. Afterwards, her pastor assured them with this promise: "We will be your family." Even when our closest relationships are strained, God's family always makes a way.

One overlooked symptom of anxiety is feeling disconnected with the people and objects around you, with a lingering sense of unreality. I experience this myself: feeling untethered, wondering what's real, pulled in the tension between my heart in heaven and my feet solidly on the ground. I never knew this was anxiety. But anytime I seek the Lord, He says something like, "You want to find me? Look around at what I've made. I'm hidden in plain sight, everywhere, *in everyone*." And His Word confirms this: "[H]e who does not love his brother whom he has seen cannot love God whom he has not seen" (1 John 4:20b). To love people is to love God, and to despise others is to be misaligned with love.

In our environment of cancel culture, conscious uncoupling, and estrangement for the sake of comfort, we must not ignore the cry for peace. Staying aligned doesn't mean we stay in harmful relationships at any cost. Instead, we work toward peace for the sake of Christ, who gave his life to reconcile us to Him and one another: "Strive for peace with everyone, and for the holiness without which no one will see the Lord" (Hebrews 12:14). Emily and her husband sought peace within their family. "My church really stepped up for us," she said. "God will make a way and He will provide people to love you. I'll happily add that we are now back in communication with [my husband's] parents. It's not perfect, but it's better. God can redeem any relationship that feels like a lost cause." Amen to that, sister.

"Strive for peace with everyone, and for the holiness without which no one will see the Lord." —Hebrews 12:14

Pretend as though you've never seen this verse. Write down "Strive for" and fill in what you'd think God would want us to strive for in pencil. Compare your answer with the promise above, and then erase yours and write the words above in pen.

_____

_____

_____

1. What relationship do you feel is out of alignment right now?

_____

_____

_____

2. "If possible, so far as it depends on you, live peaceably with all" (Romans 12:18). We do our part to create peace, and leave the rest to God. Are you doing everything in your power to live peaceably with all? Does knowing that peace doesn't always depend on you give you comfort?

_____

_____

_____

_____

3. Hebrews 12 says to "strive for peace with everyone." The Bible also encourages us to strive for rest (Hebrews 4:11) and to strive to enter through the narrow door (Luke 13:24). The word "strive" also means to "pursue aggressively," which is interesting considering the context of the verse. At the time, Christians were being persecuted, yet were encouraged to make peace with their enemies. When people revile us, we should not respond with a counter-attack, but with an eager effort toward peace. This is the way of Jesus. How can you pursue peace with someone who seems to be against you?

_____

_____

_____

_____

_____

4. We may not be fighting people, but we do fight the enemy who tries to isolate and divide us from one another. Emily talked about putting on the armor of God every time they approached a possible conflict. The armor of God includes:

   a. The belt of truth to hold fast to as our solid grounding
   b. The breastplate of righteousness to keep us from having to prove ourselves to the other person
   c. Feet ready to bring the gospel of peace, not just to keep the peace or refrain from a fight, but to make peace
   d. Shield of faith to believe the best about that person and God's plan for them, extinguishing any triggering words or tone
   e. Helmet of salvation to remind us that we are safe in the Lord, and finally,
   f. The sword of the spirit to set you both free

   When have you experienced the armor of God protecting you and your relationships? Is there an upcoming event when you will need this prayer?

   _____

   _____

   _____

   _____

5. The "peace" Hebrews 12:14 mentions doesn't necessarily mean you agree on everything. This word was used as a common Jewish farewell, wishing health and wholeness upon the other. We cannot have peace of mind if we are at war with someone else. We pursue peace because human beings are connected by Jesus' love for us. This connection

is like quantum entanglement, a scientific concept that describes how a group of particles interact in such a way that the movement of one directly affects the state of another, no matter how much distance is put between them. How does this sense of "peace" from the verse change your view about what expectations you have on a strained relationship?

---

6. We strive for peace with everyone, and "for the holiness without which no one will see the Lord." This "holiness" is the sanctification process, transforming us from our likeness to the image of Christ so we can have eyes to see God as He really is. Ephesians 4:31-32 says, "Let all bitterness and wrath and anger and clamor and slander be put away from you, along with all malice. Be kind to one another, tenderhearted, forgiving one another, as God in Christ forgave you." What, from this verse, are you having a hard time putting away?c

---

7. Striving for peace doesn't always mean there will be reconciliation. Sometimes walking in alignment with the

truth means walking away from a relationship for a time and entrusting it to the Lord. What do you need to strive for on your end of a strained relationship, and what can you entrust to the Lord in prayer?

_____

_____

_____

Emily prayed through her tension-filled season to ward off bitterness, and was ready to reconcile when it was time. Through prayer, God taught her she didn't have to be the "peacekeeper" but was called to be a "peacemaker." He told her the tension was temporary, and gave her the strength to say things like, "I think you're upset with me. Can we talk about this?" Our own hurt feelings often cloud our judgment about what's really going on in a relationship, but prayer gives us perspective from God who helps align us with His reality.

To become peacemakers, the best action step is prayer. Once you submit yourself to the Lord, who reconciles all things to Himself (Colossians 1:20), He will lead the way and give you wisdom and compassion.

Write a prayer for a strained relationship:

_____

_____

Spend a moment in centering prayer, allowing yourself to be at peace.

Day 4: Moving with the Seasons

We have a romanticized notion that somehow, some way, the stars will align and our life will be perfect. No more striving, no more stress, just peaceful bliss. I remember watching my sister wait for a tumultuous relationship to sort itself out. She was on and off with a guy from high school for six years. They were the perfect couple on paper; in fact, part of the reason she stayed was because everyone said how great they were for each other. But something wasn't clicking. "It was so much work—like trying to fit a square peg into a round hole," she said, looking back on that experience. "I felt uneasy about the future, but I didn't know how to pinpoint it at the time." When a relationship, a job, a decision feels uneasy, we can follow the still, quiet voice of the Lord leading us.

We are bound to have seasons that feel dark and uncertain. When we don't know which direction to take, look to the natural rhythms of creation and see that God has organized the days and seasons to bring life. This includes us: "Let us know; let us press on to know the Lord; his going out is sure as the dawn; he will come to us as the showers, as the spring rains that water the earth" (Hosea 6:3). May we be like watchmen waiting for the morning, and as sure as the earth turns on its axis, we will return to the light. As we watch and wait, we will see His plans for us.

Instead of trying to force what didn't work, my sister found peace in letting go and is now happily married with a sweet family of her own. I asked my sister what she would tell her high school self in that past relationship: "I would tell myself to enjoy the season I'm in and stop rushing the unknown. Looking back, I can see God had a complete plan for me. All the struggles I went through really are part of a plan. I wish I would have relied on God more and his plan for my life. But going through the struggles makes it that much sweeter in the end. I can't ask for a better life." In her story, and ours, take heart: God is working all things for good. It may take time for God's redemption in your life to play out, but trust the process. As we follow God, He will align every season with His will for us. Jesus was and is still the light of the world. In every season, may we press through the dark unknown, and persevere to know the Lord no matter what. Let's take joy in leaving our anxieties behind and moving with the seasons in the promise of peace with God.

"Let us know; let us press on to know the Lord; his going out is sure as the dawn; he will come to us as the showers, as the spring rains that water the earth." —Hosea 6:3

Write down the promise below. Take note of how your pen presses into the paper, and feel the surface pressing back. Compare this biofeedback exercise to pressing in to the Lord and receiving His response.

_____

_____

_____

_____

_____

1. Talk about a time when the Lord brought you through a season of hardship. How did that experience strengthen your faith in God? Could that event serve as a reminder that He is with you, even as you read these words?

_____

_____

_____

_____

2. The sun and moon are daily signs that God is with us. The Psalmist compares these heavenly bodies to faithful guarantees of God's covenant with us: "Like the moon it shall be established forever, a faithful witness in the skies" (Psalm 89:37). How does nature reveal the consistent presence and steadfast love of the Lord to you?

_____

_____

_____

_____

3. Our verse today encourages us to "press on to know the Lord." The context for this verse is God sending the prophet Hosea to the Israelites to encourage them to return to Him. They committed sins attributed to a lack of knowledge in God, and consistently failed to be faithful to His laws. These

actions led to the Israelites' destruction (Hosea 4:1, 6). In Christ, we are no longer punished for our sins, but we do experience the consequences, which serve as a wake-up call to come to our senses. God's kindness leads us to repentance! Even when we do not acknowledge God, his love is as sure as the sunrise: "Its rising is from the end of the heavens, and its circuit to the end of them, and there is nothing hidden from its heat" (Psalm 19:6). Are you experiencing the consequence of sin? How has God continued to extend kindness toward you?

_____

_____

_____

4. Hosea 6:2 continues with a spine-tingling prophecy: "After two days he will revive us; on the third day he will raise us up, that we may live before him." He does not call us to anything He has not already committed to. Our aim is to be reunited, realigned in sweet communion with our Lord and Savior. It's always darkest before the dawn. What are you despairing about in this season of life? How can the pattern of Jesus' death and resurrection, winter yielding to spring, and the night making way for the dawn give you hope that there is not only an end to your season, but light on the other side?

_____

_____

_____

_____

_____

5. Hosea 6:3 sends an invitation with a promise: "Let us know; let us press on to know the Lord; his going out is sure as the dawn; he will come to us as the showers, as the spring rains that water the earth." Notice this verse doesn't encourage us to press through every hard season just for the sake of surviving. What does Hosea ask us all to press on to know? How can this be your focus during your current season?

_____

_____

_____

_____

6. Hosea 6:6 lays down God's hopes for us through every season: "For I desire steadfast love and not sacrifice, the knowledge of God rather than burnt offerings." You don't have to be anxious about how you have to perform. God has not required this of you. What is his heart for you instead?

_____

_____

_____

_____

7. Peace is knowing you don't have to rush through one season of life to get to the next, but seeing the purpose where you are. In John 4:35 Jesus points out: "Do you not say, 'There are yet four months, then comes the harvest'? Look, I tell you, lift up your eyes, and see that the fields are white for harvest." We must be able to discern spiritual seasons. Knowing there is a time for everything (Ecclesiastes 3) will help us manage expectations and get aligned with God's plans instead of trying to force a different outcome. What, do you believe, is God's greater purpose for this season of your life?

_____

_____

_____

_____

   Martin Luther's first thesis in the Reformation was: "When our Lord and Master Jesus Christ said, 'Repent,' he willed the entire life of believers to be one of repentance." As every season turns, may it continue to turn us toward Christ. May we return to His promises in worship, let the worthless things pass away, and make us whole. The best rhythm built in for repentance is the Sabbath. Every week, take one day off from striving and submit to God's reign over the earth. May this day of rest open a space for the peace of God's presence to dwell in your heart. Live from that place this week, and start anew the next.

Write a brief prayer based on today's reflections. Circle a word from that prayer, and sit with it in centering prayer.

_____

_____

_____

Day 5: Let's Review

Prompt: What can you do? What's one humble step you can take with God?

Promise: *"Let us know; let us press on to know the Lord; his going out is sure as the dawn; he will come to us as the showers, as the spring rains that water the earth." —Hosea 6:3*

Recap + Quick Quotes:

For our final session together, we put everything we have learned into action. We are centered in what we know and have left behind the weight of sin and shame. This week, we take a step forward freely, humbly, as peacemakers, knowing that every step serves to increase our knowledge of Christ and the peace He gives.

- "We do not let fear and anxiety rule, but let God's Word reign and go forth."
- "Walking with humility is trusting God with our boundaries, experiencing the joy of freedom within them, and having peace that comes with the wholeness of knowing Christ."
- "[We] work toward peace as far as it depends on us for the sake of Christ, who gave his life to reconcile us to Him and one another."
- "In every season, may we press through the dark, and on to know the Lord! Let's take joy in leaving our anxieties behind, and move with the seasons in the promise of peace with God."

Group Discussion Questions:

a. *Main question:* What's one thing that has clicked with you and God this week? How have you experienced His peace in light of this week's study?

b. *Day 1:* What anxious thoughts are holding you back from something potentially life-changing? What is that anxiety saying?

c. *Day 2:* Some activities release joy and energy, and some drain us. What symptoms alert you that you are pushing past the threshold of your window of tolerance? What activities or situations encourage you and expand your tolerance, and which ones cause you to shrink back?

d. *Day 3:* When have you experienced the armor of God protecting you and your relationships? When will you need to pray this prayer next?

e. *Day 4:* What do you believe is God's greater purpose for this season of your life?

f. *Bonus question:* What doubts most often plague your mind about belief in God and what He says to be true?

Prayer:

Lord,

Let us not shrink from what is good and right and true. Let us walk humbly with God, doing justice and loving mercy. Not for our sake, but for Your name and our joy. We let You lead the way. Instead of rushing forward in haste or falling back with indecision, we make space to let you lead. You say Your temple is to be a house of prayer, so clear the tables of compromise and give us a whole heart and clear steps. We make space for you here in the next few minutes. [Let two minutes pass.] Amen.

Group Prayer Requests

_____

_____

_____

Epilogue

This is the story of the three chiropractors.

Once upon a time, there was a woman whose back hurt so badly that she went from doctor to doctor, but could find no relief. A friend suggested a chiropractor. She was skeptical, but the probability of being pain-free triumphed. Chiropractor number one said, "Your body is already good at healing, and my job is simply to restore the flow and communication through spinal adjustment." Something clicked in her spirit. Chiropractor number two released an emotion through a series of questions and prayer. Her right hip unlocked. Her eyes were opened. Chiropractor number three was a complete stranger in a hotel gym, and gave her a simple physical exercise that provided relief whenever she did it. She was to be chiropractor number four, the next messenger to bring alignment. She would not be a chiropractor in the traditional sense, but in the spiritual sense.

This time, she was to be the feet of good news, the publisher of peace, the one who drew others back into the flock. God spoke to her through these three experiences, and it was time for her to align others with His perfect peace.

If you've experienced alignment with the perfect peace that God has for you through these words, now it's your turn. There are many ways you can bring the good news. I trust that the Lord will equip you to do His will, and make His joy complete! If you need a deeper dive or want to share this message with friends, don't forget about the video teachings at **joyfulhealth.co/aligned**.

Before you go, would you complete my joy and respond to what you've received in this study? Most of this writing process involves me talking to you in faith that you'll hear and receive the gift that God has for you in this message. ***The best gift would be for you to write a review on Amazon or send me a message on Instagram @kaseybshuler. I can't wait to hear from you!***

"Now may the Lord of peace himself give you peace at all times in every way. The Lord be with you all." 2 Thessalonians 3:16

Appendix

Aligned Quick Steps

To sum up what to do when you're uncertain, **focus on what you can do and pray about the rest.** Use these quick steps based on the study to return to God's perfect peace when you're anxious and misaligned:

Prompt	Promise
When you feel pulled in every direction or unsure of which way to go, remember who you are.	*"But now thus says the Lord, he who created you, O Jacob, he who formed you, O Israel: 'Fear not, for I have redeemed you; I have called you by name, you are mine.'" Isaiah 43:1*
Remind yourself that perfect peace starts with God.	*"You keep him in perfect peace whose mind is stayed on you, because he trusts in you" Isaiah 26:3*

Know there are steps to return to alignment with the Lord.	*"I have said these things to you, that in me you may have peace. In the world you will have tribulation. But take heart; I have overcome the world." John 16:33*
Name what you do not know. Bring up these questions in prayer to the Lord and be held in the mystery.	*"The secret things belong to the Lord our God, but the things that are revealed belong to us and to our children forever, that we may do all the words of this law." Deuteronomy 29:29*
What do you know? Live your life on the promises of God you know to be true.	*"Do not be anxious about anything, but in everything by prayer and supplication with thanksgiving let your requests be made known to God. And the peace of God, which surpasses all understanding, will guard your hearts and your minds in Christ Jesus" — Philippians 4:6-7*
What can you let go of? What is not yours to own and entrust to God?	*"But the meek shall inherit the land and delight themselves in abundant peace." —Psalm 37:11*
What can you do? What's one humble step you can take with God?	*"Let us know; let us press on to know the Lord; his going out is sure as the dawn; he will come to us as the showers, as the spring rains that water the earth." —Hosea 6:3*

Pray the Promises of God for Anxiety

When praying the promises of God, have confidence in these three things and say:

- **Your will**: God's promises are His will for us, so we know when we pray His promises that He will answer: "And this is the confidence that we have toward him, that if we ask anything according to his will he hears us" (1 John 5:14).
- **Your peace:** When you're anxious, God promises His peace with prayer: "do not be anxious about anything, but in everything by prayer and supplication with thanksgiving let your requests be made known to God. And the peace of God, which surpasses all understanding, will guard your hearts and your minds in Christ Jesus" (Philippians 4:6-7).
- **Your way, your time:** We do not know exactly when or how God will fulfill His promises, but we can have assurance that He will be true to Himself so we can ask confidently in prayer: "if we are faithless, he remains faithful—for he cannot deny himself" (2 Timothy 2:13).

When you're anxious about being **alone**, God promises He is always with you:

- *"Keep your life free from love of money, and be content with what you have, for he has said, 'I will never leave you nor forsake you.'"* —Hebrews 13:5

- *"For I am sure that neither death nor life, nor angels nor rulers, nor things present nor things to come, nor powers, nor height nor depth, nor anything else in all creation, will be able to separate us from the love of God in Christ Jesus our Lord."* —Romans 8:38-39

When what we have or who we are doesn't feel **enough**: "But he said to me, *'My grace is sufficient for you, for my power is made perfect in weakness.' Therefore I will boast all the more gladly of my weaknesses, so that the power of Christ may rest upon me."* —2 Corinthians 12:9

When you need **guidance**: *"The Lord is my shepherd; I shall not want."* —Psalm 23:1

When you're anxious about your **faith**: Jesus promises that He will return for us: *"In my Father's house are many rooms. If it were not so, would I have told you that I go to prepare a place for you? And if I go and prepare a place for you, I will come again and will take you to myself, that where I am you may be also. And you know the way to where I am going."* —John 14:2-4

When you're anxious about your **future**, God promises that He will work things out for His children: *"And we know that for those who love God all things work together for good, for those who are called according to his purpose."* —Romans 8:28

When nothing seems to **last**:

"The grass withers, the flower fades, but the word of our God will stand forever." —Isaiah 40:8

"Oh give thanks to the Lord, for he is good; for his steadfast love endures forever!" —Psalm 118:29

When you're anxious about the **news** of doom and gloom, Jesus promises to give us life to the full: *"The thief comes only to steal and kill and destroy. I came that they may have life and have it abundantly."* —John 10:10

When we aren't sure what's **possible**: *"I can do all things through him who strengthens me."* —Philippians 4:13

When you're anxious about **provision,** God promises He will provide for our needs:

- *"But seek first the kingdom of God and his righteousness, and all these things will be added to you."* —Matthew 6:33
- *"And my God will supply every need of yours according to his riches in glory in Christ Jesus."* —Philippians 4:19
- *"Look at the birds of the air: they neither sow nor reap nor gather into barns, and yet your heavenly Father feeds them. Are you not of more value than they?"* —Matthew 6:26

When you're anxious about **rest**, Jesus promises rest when we come to Him: *"Come to me, all who labor and are heavy laden, and I will give you rest. Take my yoke upon you, and learn from me, for I am gentle and lowly in heart, and you will find rest for your souls. For my yoke is easy, and my burden is light."* —Matthew 11:28-30

When you are fearful of being **sad**: *"Those who sow in tears shall reap with shouts of joy!"* —Psalm 126:5

When we don't feel **safe**: *"He who dwells in the shelter of the Most High will abide in the shadow of the Almighty."* —Psalm 91:1

When you're anxious about falling short and losing your **salvation**: *"My sheep hear my voice, and I know them, and they follow me. I give them eternal life, and they will never perish, and no one will snatch them out of my hand. My Father, who has given them to me, is greater than all, and no one is able to snatch them out of the Father's hand."* —John 10:27-29

When you're not sure who will be **saved**: *"For God so loved the world, that he gave his only Son, that whoever believes in him should not perish but have eternal life."* —John 3:16

When you're anxious and **scared**, God promises to be with us: *"So do not fear, for I am with you; do not be dismayed, for I am your God. I will strengthen you and help you; I will uphold you with my righteous right hand."* —Isaiah 41:10, NIV

When you're not sure if you will **succeed**: *"Commit your work to the Lord, and your plans will be established."* —Proverbs 16:3

When you're anxious about a **sin or wrongdoing**, *God promises to forgive us: "If we confess our sins, he is faithful and just to forgive us our sins and to cleanse us from all unrighteousness."* —1 John 1:9

When we are worried about not having the **strength** to keep going: *"They who wait for the Lord shall renew their strength."* — Isaiah 40:31

When we are anxious about **suffering,** God promises to comfort us and use our affliction to be a blessing to others who are suffering: *"Blessed be the God and Father of our Lord Jesus Christ, the Father of mercies and God of all comfort, who comforts us in all our affliction, so that we may be able to comfort those who are in any affliction, with the comfort with which we ourselves are comforted by God."* —2 Corinthians 1:3-4

When you are worried about an upcoming **trial**: *"When you pass through the waters, I will be with you; and through the rivers, they shall not overwhelm you; when you walk through fire you shall not be burned, and the flame shall not consume you."* —Isaiah 43:2

When you've lost **trust** in all others: *"Let us hold fast the confession of our hope without wavering, for he who promised is faithful."* —Hebrews 10:23

When you do not feel **valued**: *"Humble yourselves before the Lord, and he will exalt you."* —James 4:10

When you don't know which **way** to take: *"Jesus said to him, 'I am the way, and the truth, and the life. No one comes to the Father except through me.'"* —John 14:6

When you're not sure **who you are**:
- *"See what kind of love the Father has given to us, that we should be called children of God; and so we are. The*

reason why the world does not know us is that it did not know him." —1 John 3:1

- *"No, in all these things we are more than conquerors through him who loved us."* —Romans 8:37

Find More Support for Anxiety

If anxiety is interfering with your everyday life, please consult a trusted health professional or call the National Alliance on Mental Illness (NAMI) at 1-800-950-NAMI (6264). If you are in a crisis or looking for mental health information, you can call NAMI's helpline for free support.

Acknowledgements

Thank you to my beta readers for their invaluable feedback, specifically Megan Little, Pinky Harper, and Emily Werger. You kept me on track, kept me company, and shared with me the riches of God's grace week-to-week.

Thank you to my editor, Susan Hobbs, for not only understanding me, but shaping these words into what they are today.

Thank you to my family for always grounding me in what matters, allowing this book to be an overflow of the love in my life.

And thank you to Jesus, who is my peace.

My stenghts

- discipline
- organized
- honest
- obedient
- good at sports (gift from GOD)
- responsable
-

my weakness

- fearful
- negative thinking (pesimist)
- judgemental
- overthinking
-

Made in the USA
Columbia, SC
03 April 2023

14730536R00126